BULLS, BIRDIES, BOGEYS & BEARS

The Remarkable & Revealing Relationship Between Golf & Investment Markets.

W0008049

KEVIN ARMSTRONG
Foreword by Sir Bob Charles

Published by:

Wilkinson Publishing Pty Ltd ACN 006 042 173

Level 4, 2 Collins Street Melbourne, Victoria, Australia 3000

Ph: +61 3 9654 5446

www.wilkinsonpublishing.com.au

National Library of Australia Cataloguing-in-Publication data:

Author: Armstrong, Kevin John.

Title: Bulls, birdies, bogeys & bears : the remarkable & revealing

          relationship between golf & investment markets / Kevin Armstrong.

ISBN: 9781921804960 (pbk.)

Subjects: Investments.

          Golf.

Dewey Number: 332.6

Photos and illustrations by agreement with international agencies, photographers and illustrators from Getty Images.

Design: Michael Bannenberg.

Printed in China.

FOREWORD
By Sir Bob Charles

Having travelled the world to play competitive golf at the highest level for more than fifty years it is fair to say that I have had the privilege and honour to meet, and in some cases compete, with many of the illustrious names covered throughout *Bulls, Birdies, Bogeys and Bears*, including Warren Buffett. However, despite competing for so many years, and fortunately witnessing a lot of what is now considered golf history first hand, I had never considered that a relationship such as that presented in this book could exist. But now it is clear that it does as the reader will soon discover.

My professional career began in the very early sixties and extended, thanks to the US Senior Tour, through more than five decades, and as I review the various stages of my own career I can start to see how some of the ebb and flow of the markets has been reflected in golf and vice versa. I benefited from the emergence of 'The Big Three', Palmer, Player and Nicklaus, and the boom that accompanied their heyday. In 1969 I was playing with Tony Jacklin when he won at Royal Lytham & St. Annes to become the first Briton in almost twenty years to win The Open and his victory was huge for British golf. As one reflects upon these events it becomes obvious that professional golf does not exist, nor can it prosper, in isolation.

Later in my career, at 50, I was indeed fortunate to become eligible for what is now known as The Champions Tour which coincided with the rampant bull market that ran throughout the nineties and peaked in 2000. That bull market was obvious on the PGA Tour but it was even more apparent on the Champions Tour. The leading money winner in 1998, Hale Irwin, won more than thirty times the money that Miller Barber had in 1981, the year before the bull market began, and he won more than David Duval did in topping the PGA Tour money list.

I have always had an interest in golf and its history and since returning to New Zealand, and competing and travelling less, I have taken a greater interest in investment markets and what drives them.

By coincidence, at the time I retired to New Zealand, a friend and neighbour asked me to make up a four at Clearwater Golf Club with Kevin Armstrong. Whilst sharing a ride with Kevin around Clearwater that day it was clear that not only was he an able golfer, he also displayed a remarkable interest in golf history. As it happened, that evening Kevin was making one of his regular investment presentations to clients in Christchurch which I decided to attend. It was quickly apparent that his interest in history was not limited to golf as he discussed investment markets and their prospects in a manner that I had not witnessed before.

In his presentations and writings Kevin displays a strong irreverence for economists in general and conventional wisdom in particular, while at the same time paying a great deal of respect to history.

In *Bulls Birdies Bogeys and Bears* Kevin draws on his knowledge of both golf and investment markets and convincingly shows that they are related in a manner that, to the best of my knowledge, is unique and far beyond the realm of coincidence.

Sir Bob Charles
Clearwater, Christchurch
New Zealand
October 2012

CONTENTS

INTRODUCTION
The "Great Games"

"Golf is typical capitalist lunacy." George Bernard Shaw

A close relationship has existed between business and golf since golf began. However, over the last century, this remarkable connection has grown ever closer.

To some extent the reason for this relationship is understandable. Business and business relationships can be developed and grown on the golf course. This is not true of any other sport. The pace, style and handicapping system of golf uniquely allows participants the opportunity to compete against each other, yet at the same time converse and get to know one another. Golf is a game of honesty and integrity and this leads many business people to believe they learn more of the character of a colleague, client or employee in one round of golf than in any number of meetings or interviews

All these aspects of "The Great Game", as golf has frequently been described, mean that the two activities, golf and business, are inextricably linked. *Bulls, Birdies, Bogeys and Bears* explores these links from a historic, current and future perspective. However, this relationship's most intriguing manifestation is that evidenced in the behaviour of many of the measures of the "pulse" of both business and golf.

The most obvious pulse of business is found in the ever-changing mood and level of stock markets. The pulse of golf is harder to measure. However, *Bulls, Birdies, Bogeys and Bears* reveals and explores several such measures, as well as many more anecdotal indicators.

These indicators illustrate that the movements and developments, growth and contraction, of both activities have been, and will likely continue to be, closely correlated, and to a far greater extent than any other sport and certainly more than mere coincidence could account for.

Investing, at least on Wall Street, has also been known as "The Great Game". Both golf and investing require a similar self-discipline and single mindedness. Both are at the same time absorbing and frustrating, and can become either a healthy obsession or a damaging addiction. However, the greatest truth about both activities is that they are highly complex and neither can ever be conquered. The moment a participant starts to think they have mastered "it", they can be assured of being very quickly disabused of any such notion. Both great games are endlessly humbling.

The emotional highs and lows that both golf and investing induce, and the need to keep those emotions controlled, is one of the threads that link them. These emotional swings must be managed not only for the split second that playing a shot or placing a trade may take, but also over much longer periods where doubts and fears have plenty of time to grow. There are few other sports where the competitor must stay focused, yet calm, in the face of a myriad of obstacles and challenges, dealing with moments of extreme joy and agony over potentially a four-day period or, at least, a four-hour round. Similarly, inner strength and fortitude, over timeframes ranging from seconds to days and even years, is essential in investing if success is to be achieved.

The emotional similarity between the two great games may be the underlying root of their incredible interconnectedness – a connection not seen between investing and any other sport. There are, however, many other potential causes on many different levels. Understanding and highlighting this relationship lies at the heart of *Bulls, Birdies, Bogeys and Bears*.

It is unlikely that *Bulls, Birdies, Bogeys and Bears* will make either a poor golfer a good golfer or a poor investor a good investor. However, looking at golf from an investing perspective, and investing from a golfing perspective, may provide some insights into why one may have shortcomings in either endeavour. It is not a "how to" book on golf or investing, nor is it an explanation as to why the remarkable link exists between these two great games and it may pose more questions than it answers. However, what is almost certain is, that while the various "pulses" of golf and investing may have moved in a highly correlated manner, their relationship is neither coincidence, nor is it evidence of either one being cause or effect. Rather both are merely symptoms of broader movements in collective social mood. Nonetheless, an appreciation for this close relationship may lead readers to their own conclusions as to what movements in markets may mean for golf, or what shifts in future trends in golf may imply about investment markets and business.

Back in the early 1930s, the venerable golf-writer Bernard Darwin described in *Out of the Rough* the first surge in both the popularity, and the general appreciation of skill, in golf. He was describing the emergence of the "Great Triumvirate" – J H Taylor, James Braid and Harry Vardon – in the last years of the 19th century. These three players dominated golf and the populace's imagination like few sportsmen had before. They took golf to a new, previously incomprehensible, level and, to quote Darwin, the game was "booming".

It is one of the contentions of *Bulls, Birdies, Bogeys and Bears* that golf booms when business and stock markets are booming. It further appears that when golf is really booming it finds a new hero, or even a trio of heroes as in the "Great Triumvirate" and sixty years later the "Big Three" of Palmer, Nicklaus and Player. It may appear that it is the new star, or stars, that create the boom in golf, or it may just seem coincidence that business, markets and golf all boom as the star emerges. What is more likely is that coincident booms in markets and golf facilitate the emergence of a star. It would be very challenging to be considered a true star, and to capture the public's imagination, if your sport was in decline amidst a souring social mood, no matter how good one was.

It is therefore both intriguing and enlightening to see just how often these "coincidences", between golf and the markets, have occurred.

The late 19th century was a period of economic and scientific importance. There was a great deal of excitement about the dawning of a new century, the British Empire was at its peak and the world was being propelled forward on a wave of new inventions, from electrification to the telephone. This was reflected in the stock markets of the time as a new wave of speculation emerged. So, just as golf was enjoying its first widely documented boom – along with the requisite new cadre of stars – investment markets and the economy were also booming.

By the early days of the 20th century, British domination of business, and possibly the world, was coming to an end as America emerged from its colonial past. This was beginning to be seen in the relative performance of the two powers' stock markets and would eventually be seen on the golf course too.

A powerful confirmation that Britain was on the decline came in the US Open of 1913. Then a little known former caddie, Francis Ouimet, saw off the might of British golf in winning the Championship amid immensely trying conditions. From then on the tide had turned and America began to take on the mantle of the world's dominant stock market, economy and golfing nation.

Golf certainly blossomed during the twenties, particularly in America, and the great amateur Bobby Jones was no small part of this growth. After the Great Triumvirate, he was the next truly dominant player. Again, an explosion in golf was coincident with a booming economy, a surging stock market and the arrival of a new 'star'.

This state of affairs lasted until the early- nineteen thirties and the onset of the Great Depression. While the Great Depression was a global phenomenon, it hit America particularly hard, and the US stock market reflected this. So too did golf. No American won the British Open for fourteen years from 1933 onwards, having previously dominated the event for more than the prior decade.

While golf remained popular, its growth was overshadowed by the gloom of World War II. However, after the war golf emerged with a bang and so did the stock market. One of the world's most enduring bull markets was just in its infancy, and a new breed of golfing star was emerging. The crescendo of this bull market was seen when golf was brought literally into everyone's living rooms by the miracle of television and the American public embraced its swashbuckling new hero, Arnold Palmer. To this day, his name is still one of the most recognised, admired and loved in golf. And when he was joined in the early 1960s by Gary Player and Jack Nicklaus as the "Big Three" – the modern day triumvirate – golf exploded on the upside and so did the markets.

Despite Gary Player being a South African, golf in the 1960s and 1970s was dominated by America. Ryder Cup results through this period clearly show the one-sided nature of world golf at the time. However, things were beginning to change by the 1980s. Globalisation in investing was being discussed at the same time as golf was also embracing globalisation. Courses were being opened where, just a few years earlier, no one had even heard of golf. The decade of Japan had arrived.

If an investor had perfect foresight he would have easily seen this coming. The Japanese stock market was set to explode on the upside through the 1980s. And it was not just the stock market – real estate soared along with most other assets in Japan. Swept up in this wave, and possibly even leading it, was golf. Golf club memberships in Japan became one of the most sought-after investments, and the money available for Japanese golfers on the Japanese tour soared. American golf did not slide backwards in the 80s, but in comparison to Japan it felt like it did.

Through the late 1980s, as the US markets struggled to recover from the 87 crash, investors' appetites for global investing grew and the number of markets open to international investors expanded to meet this demand. At the same time, golf's dominant superstar, Greg Norman proposed a world tour, picking up on an earlier idea of Arnold Palmer's. Greg was ahead of his time by about a decade.

New trends in anything often begin with a false start. This was seen with the emergence of American golf and its stock market prior to the 1929 crash and the Great Depression. Both suffered terribly through that period only to re-emerge with even greater strength fifteen years later. The globalisation of both golf and investing followed a similar path.

Through the 1990s, the US once again became the world's dominant economy, stock market, and eventually the birthplace of great golfers.

In the 1980s and very early 1990s, the US wanted to be more like Japan. Then, the emerging markets of Asia took over the baton of growth after Japan's bubble had burst. America must have wondered what it could do in the face of these "Tiger" economies. Eventually, after the Asian crisis, the US did once again become the world's growth engine, and its stock market the world's best performing. In an unlikely and humorous coincidence, America also had the next great golf star. America became a "Tiger" at the same time as Tiger (Woods) began to rewrite the record books.

The world is certainly more global now. The world's best golfers play virtually a global tour, and the undisputed global golf star, Tiger Woods, is, while American by birth, a truly multicultural and global athlete.

The last century began with golf booming on the back of a new wave of golfing stars known as the Great Triumvirate and amidst a surge in innovation and development. Over the subsequent century, golf's popularity and fortunes, and that of its professional participants, have been closely linked with the ebb and flow of global stock markets. It is highly probable that this will continue to be the case going forward.

What is harder to foretell is whether Tiger's winning more majors will ensure that markets continue to rise, or whether rising markets will guarantee even greater popularity for golf. The answer is most likely a mixture of these and other imponderables that could each fill a book by themselves.

Bulls, Birdies, Bogeys and Bears does not make any specific forecasts. However, after reading *Bulls, Birdies, Bogeys and Bears*, one may look at both activities in a slightly different light and enjoy the endless challenges and pleasures of each more than one might have otherwise.

It is not the intention of *Bulls, Birdies, Bogeys and Bears* to forecast who will win the next major, what continents may dominate golf, how golf may grow or contract or what regional and global stock markets may do. Rather, *Bulls, Birdies, Bogeys and Bears* observes and comments upon the clear link that exists between golf and investing. There is no presumption of either activity being cause or effect. In fact it is almost certain that movements in both are the result of larger trends in the economy and society. That being said, the history of the connection is fascinating and there seems to be no reason to doubt that it will continue.

CHAPTER ONE
How close and for how long?

"The main purpose of the stock market is to make fools of as many men as possible."
Bernard Baruch
"Golf is so popular simply because it is the best game in the world at which to be bad."
A. A. Milne

The central thesis of *Bulls, Birdies, Bogeys and Bears* is that golf and the business world, particularly as measured by the stock market, are closely related. This chapter explores the actual evidence of this close relationship.

The genesis of the idea behind this book came from observations regarding the staggering growth in money won by professional golfers over the last few decades, and how the possibly egregious sums paid to players in the "great game" of golf were analogous to the amounts paid to corporate chief executives and successful participants in the other "great game", the stock market.

In exploring the relationship between these two activities, it quickly becomes apparent that they are very closely linked. It is not simply a matter of there being a lot of money at stake in both "games". Rather, it is that the very "pulse" of each activity – their ebb and flow – are synchronised.

The pulse of business is easily measured through the stock market. The actions of the Dow Jones Industrial Average, the S&P 500 or the NASDAQ are continuously announced and analysed throughout the media tick-by-tick, year-by-year, and on an even longer basis. The pulse of golf is harder to measure, and is naturally somewhat more subjective than the level of an index. One such yardstick, however, is the amount of money won on tour by the sport's leading players.

To some extent the reason for the relationship is understandable. Business can be conducted on the golf course and business relationships can be developed and grown on the golf course. This is not true of any other sport. Golf is a game of honesty and integrity. It is largely self-policed and is therefore probably the easiest game in the world to cheat at, and as a result, how an individual behaves on a golf course can be highly revealing. It is for this reason, among others, that "Business Golf" is so popular. Four hours or more on a golf course can highlight both flaws and qualities in an individual that any number of psychometric tests, interviews and meetings will fail to reveal. Golf also lends itself to the building of long-term friendships and a level of mutual understanding – qualities that are so valuable in any successful business relationship.

The growth in total prize money accumulated by the world's leading golfer has largely tracked the ebb and flow of the total return of the global stock markets - their "pulses" have been similar.

That a connection exists between golf and business is both obvious and understandable. What is far less obvious is how major changes in golf have been mirrored by changes in the business world, and vice versa. The "pulse" of golf and the "pulse" of business, at least as reflected in the investment world, have been and are likely to continue to be inextricably linked.

The "pulse" of the business world, or investment markets, is relatively easy to follow. All regions of the world that have share markets publish their levels each day. The ever-changing ebb and flow of these indices is the community of investors' view of the underlying health or otherwise of these businesses. The golf world's "pulse" is somewhat harder to follow but, nonetheless, it exists, and for professional golfers money is a reasonable measure of that "pulse".

The growth in total prize money accumulated by the world's leading golfer has largely tracked the ebb and flow of the total return of the global stock markets - their "pulses" have been similar. This cannot be said of any other sport. Thirty years ago tennis players were the most highly paid athletes on the planet, and their exploits dominated the sporting media. This is not the case now. Whilst the money is still good in tennis it doesn't capture the public's imagination the way it once did and the leading exponents are relatively anonymous, at least when compared to golfing superstars who are immediately recognised just by their first names – Tiger, Rory, Phil or Luke.

Both activities challenge participants emotionally. Doubts can grow and fade over multiple time frames and a strong sense of discipline is essential if one is to succeed. It is also vital, in both fields of endeavour, that participants set strategies and goals to provide a framework and structure within which to exercise the required discipline. It is all too easy in either "great game" to be caught up by whatever may be the latest fad or whim that will supposedly provide a shortcut to success, but there are no shortcuts in either "great game".

True success in both comes from a combination of patience, discipline and humility.

It is possible that it is the psychological, emotional and behavioural nature of the challenge, so obviously present in both "great games", which can at least provide a starting point in explaining and understanding their interconnectedness.

THE PULSES

The following chart (next page) shows the last twenty-two years of price action in the Dow Jones Industrial Average compared to the amount of money won by the leading money winner on the US tour in each of those years. The scales are the same (except that three extra zeros are required on the left hand money winner's total) and superficially there is indeed a passing resemblance, however, what is most intriguing is how the year to year ebb and flow of one measure has been mirrored in the other.

The chart begins in 1990, a year that was a disappointment for the markets as they suffered their worst sell off since the 1987 crash and that crash was still very much in the forefront of investors'

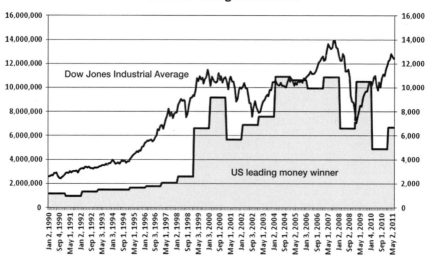

US Leading Money Winner Compared to Dow Jones Industrial Average since 1990

minds. During 1990 the leading money winner was Australian Greg Norman, the "Great White Shark", with winnings of $1.165 million, a large sum for the time. But, reflecting the more difficult market and economic conditions, Norman's total was down quite markedly from the almost $1.4 million that Tom Kite had amassed in 1989. As Kite was accumulating what was then a record haul in 1989 the US market was also on something of a roll, it rose virtually every month that year and finally broke above the level that had been achieved prior to the crash, in the summer of 1987.

The following year, 1991, the market struggled to make much headway after its recovery from the Gulf War lows in 1990, spending much of the time meandering sideways. That year Corey Pavin won the money title with a total of "only" $925,000. A modest sum compared to prior winners' totals and only about 6% more than Curtis Strange had won in the crash year of 1987. The high for the market in that crash year was 2,746, achieved in August – coincidentally, four years later, in August of Pavin's winning year, the market was also only up 6% from that level.

With the crash and the Gulf War behind it the market progressed higher through the early 1990s, but the progression was modest at best with only a very gentle rate of ascent, and almost record low levels of volatility. A similar slow and steady progression was seen among the money winners. Fred Couples topped the list in his Masters-winning year of 1992 and Nick Price won the crown in both 1993 and 1994 and each year the total was higher. However, even in 1994 Price's total of $1.5 million was only thirty percent more than Strange had won seven years earlier in 1987.

In 1995 the rate of ascent of the market and of the leading money winner's total accelerated. That year Greg Norman recaptured the title with a record total of $1.65 million and the following year Tom Lehman topped the list with almost $1.8 million. Then in 1997 Tiger Woods arrived on the scene and won the money title in his first full year on tour with more than $2 million. This was a huge increase on what had been won just a handful of years earlier but the market had risen even more dramatically. As 1997 ended the Dow was breaking through 8,000 up two hundred percent from where it had been when Corey Pavin topped the money winners in 1991.

If prize money had lagged the market through the mid-1990s it was about to catch up. In 1999 Tiger won $6.6 million and then in 2000, when the markets hit their all time high, he won more than $9 million and suddenly prize money in golf was rising faster than the market. Since the beginning of the 1990s the market had risen more than four times in value, over the same period the leading money winner on the US Tour had seen their prize winnings increase eight fold.

Both the market and the money in golf had come a long way and the increases in both had gone from being gradual and steady to ever more hyped and frenzied as the millennium approached. Unfortunately, particularly for a new breed of technology investors, the world was about to change. The technology-laden NASDAQ, whose rise in the latter half of the decade had mirrored the rise in golf prize money, peaked in March 2000 at 5,132, up 538% from the high it recorded six years earlier in

March 1994. This increase is uncannily close to the 513% increase in winnings that Tiger achieved in 2000 compared to that of Nick Price in 1994. From that peak the NASDAQ plunged, ultimately falling almost eighty percent in value over the next two and a half years as the technology, media and telecoms bubble well and truly burst.

The Dow hit its peak a couple of months earlier than the NASDAQ, but it too fell over the next two and half years, ultimately bottoming down about forty percent. The collapse in the total won by the leading money winner was just as severe and even more abrupt. After Tiger's impressive year in 2000, 2001 was something of a letdown. He "only" won five tournaments compared to the prior year's nine and while he won the money title his total of $5.7 million was, like the Dow only a bit sooner, down forty percent on his 2000 total.

From their respective low points both the market and the money winner's total rose through the 2000s. Vijay Singh set the record total for the money winners in 2004 with $10.9 million. This was almost equalled by Tiger three years later in 2007 with $10.86 million and this was the same year as the Dow recorded its all time high. That high was 14,279 in October 2007 and was twenty percent higher than the market had achieved at its 2000 high — almost exactly the same percentage increase in prize money that Tiger accumulated in 2007 compared to his 2000 total. But in late 2007, as in 2000 the world was about to change for just about everyone. The Global Financial Crisis, as it would ultimately become known, was about to begin.

Over the next year and a half the world suffered through the worst economic and stock market collapse since the Great Depression, and the Dow ultimately fell fifty-five percent in value. This time the fall in prize money took slightly longer, but it was just as severe. Money winner totals fell for the next three years finally bottoming out when Matt Kuchar topped the list in 2010 with $4.91 million, like the Dow, down exactly fifty-five percent from the 2007 peak. This was the lowest winning total since 1998 and the Dow had fallen to a level not seen since 1997.

From those depressed low points both the money winner totals and the Dow have begun to recover, at least for now, but what is clear is that over the last two decades the "pulses" of both the US market and the leading money winners on the US Tour have been moving together. This is not peculiar to the last two decades, and has actually been the case ever since money lists began.

THE LONG PULSE

The graph (below) shows the full history of the two "pulses" - the leading money winner's total since 1934 and the total return of the US stock market since that very depressed year. Over such a long time period it does make sense to look at the total return of the market, that is including dividends and assuming that they were reinvested, as over such lengthy periods the dividend return grows to become a very major portion of the total return.

The first official money winner's title was awarded for the 1934 season and it was won by the diminutive Paul Runyan, known as "Little Poison" thanks to his lack of length and astoundingly good short game. He would almost certainly have won the year before in 1933 had an

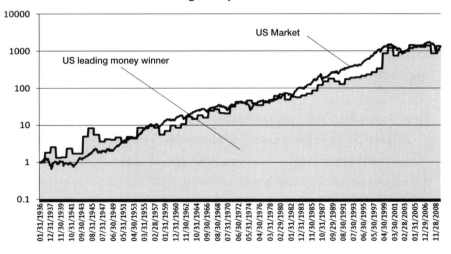

The total return of the US market compared to the US leading money winner since 1936

official list been compiled as he won a staggering eight times that year. He followed that success up with a tremendous 1934 during which he won six times, including his first of two US PGA titles and a third place in the inaugural Masters Tournament, and amassed the princely sum of $6,767. This may not sound much by today's standards, however, in the wake of the 1929 crash and at the depths of what would become known as the Great Depression, with one in five of the working population unemployed, $6,767 was almost four and a half times the average household income of just $1,524.

What is truly striking, and reflects the core thesis of this book, is that had Little Poison taken his 1934 winnings and invested it all in the US stock market, twenty years later, forty years later and even into the 2000s his wealth would have grown to almost exactly the amount that each year's leading money winner accumulated. The growth in the return from the US market over the last three quarters of a century has been identical to the growth in the amount of money that the leading golfer on the US PGA Tour has won.

This is unlikely to be mere coincidence, and certainly hasn't been the case with other sports, as will be illustrated later in this chapter, but just as the ebb and flow in the growth of these two "pulses" have been echoes of each other since 1990 the same is true since Paul Runyan's banner year.

Over the eight seasons that followed Little Poison's initial money winner's title, the leading money winners' haul made little net progress, rather it swung around in a very volatile range, despite some outstanding play from superstars of the era like Ben Hogan and Sam Snead. Snead won the title in 1938 with a then record total of more than $19,000 and eight victories, but then two years later Ben Hogan won what would be his first of three titles in a row and four in total with only a little over half that amount.

A volatile trading range could describe what the leading money winners experienced from 1936 through to 1942 when Hogan won with a total of just over $13,000 and it could also describe what the

Dow Jones Industrial Average endured in that post-Depression pre-War period. From 1936 the Dow rallied thirty percent, then fell by fifty percent, rallied by more than fifty percent before finally plunging by forty percent to its post-Pearl Harbour lows in the first half of 1942. From that very depressed low point the market embarked on what would ultimately be seen as its longest bull market ever (finally ending in 1966), but over just the next four years the market rose in a virtually uninterrupted fashion by more than one hundred percent. An even more dramatic breakout was seen in the fortunes of professional golfers.

In the wake of the Pearl Harbour attack and the entry of the United States into World War II, organised professional golf virtually evaporated in 1943. From a peak in 1938 of thirty-eight events and more than $150,000 in total prize money there were only three events held in 1943, no majors and only $17,000 was up for grabs, and as a result no official records as to who won what were compiled. This all changed in 1944, the year Byron Nelson began writing the record books. With a backdrop of rising markets Nelson dominated the tour in a way no one ever had before. He won eight of the twenty-two events held that year, including a then record three in a row, and accumulated just under $38,000 in total prize money, more than a quarter of all the money available and almost twice as much as any golfer had ever won in a single year. If 1944 had been a decent year in the market and a very good year for Byron Nelson, 1945 was going to be even better for both the market and Nelson and for professional golfers in general.

1945 saw the Dow rise virtually every month and by about thirty percent in total, finally surpassing the level it had achieved in 1937. At the same time the lot of professional golfers was improving. Amongst the majors only the US PGA was held, won by Nelson, but the tour did expand to thirty-six events, the most since the late 1930s, and more importantly the prize money at stake exploded to more than $435,000, almost three times the total of the previous year. Of that total Nelson won fifteen percent, a massive $63,336 easily surpassing his record of the previous year. While his money-winning total is impressive, and it set a record that would not be bettered until Bob Toski in 1954, it was how he accumulated the total that warrants greater attention. Nelson in 1945 produced the greatest display of consistent excellence that has ever been seen in golf and possibly any sport. Of the thirty-six official events he won eighteen of them including eleven in a row (easily beating his record of three set in 1944). In fact he actually won twelve in a row but one of them was unofficial as its purse of $2,500 was below the PGA's then minimum of $3,000. In addition to the eighteen wins Nelson was runner-up seven times that year, a truly exceptional feat and one that is unlikely to ever be surpassed. It may be thought that being a war year Nelson was competing against a weakened field, however, both Sam Snead (6) and Ben Hogan (5) were also multiple winners on tour in 1945.

After Nelson's historic 1945 achievements both golf and the markets fell into something of the doldrums. The Dow did struggle to a slightly higher level in early 1946 but then rolled over and, in September of that year, suffered a mini crash, falling twelve percent and ultimately hitting a low the following year, twenty-five percent below the 1946 high. That range was not materially broken until the recession lows of mid-1949 (on the downside) and then, on the high side, by the recovery in the market in 1950. That period of frustration and pain for investors was also experienced by professional golfers. From the 1945 high in both total purse available and the number of tournaments the tour struggled, hitting bottom, coincidentally, in 1949. That year there were only twenty-five official events, down from thirty-six in Nelson's record year, and the total purse available from those events fell more than twenty-two percent, to just $338,200. Sam Snead, with six wins including the Masters and the US PGA, topped the 1949 money winners list, but with less than half the total that Nelson won in 1945.

The US market's deep recession-induced low in mid-1949 proved to be an important bottom. After four years of making no progress the market began a seven-year advance that would deliver investors gains of more than one hundred and thirty percent before faltering in mid-1956 and falling through most of 1957. Over that same period the total prize money on tour grew by an almost identical amount rising to a total of $847,070 and the leading money winner's take also grew, and again by an almost identical amount. In 1956 Ted Kroll, a highly decorated war veteran with three purple hearts, topped the money list. He won three events and was runner up in the PGA to Jack Burke Jr and earned a then record $72,836 in prize money, one hundred and thirty percent more than Snead received in 1949.

In 1957 markets suffered their worst fall in a decade, dropping about twenty percent into the 1957/8 recession lows at the end of the year. Total prize money on tour slipped slightly that year, the first decline in total prize money since the late 1940s, and so too did the take of the leading money winner, Dick Mayer, who won about ten percent less than Kroll had in 1956. While Mayer may have been the leading money winner that year, 1957 was most memorable for the emergence of the player that would ultimately be known simply as "The King", Arnold Palmer. He had turned pro in 1954 after winning that year's US Amateur and won his first tournament in 1955. The following year he won two and then in 1957 he won four events, more than any other player.

Markets recovered from that low point at the end of 1957 and so too did professional golf. Total prize money rose twenty percent and seven more tournaments were played but 1958 really marked the start of the Palmer era. That year he topped the money list, won three more tournaments, importantly including his first professional major, the Masters Tournament. By the end of the year the market had risen thirty percent. In 1959 total prize money again grew by twenty percent and the market continued to rise hitting its peak at the end of the year, up about fifteen percent. Palmer again had a good year, winning three times, but the money title went to Art Wall Jnr who enjoyed the best year of his career. He won four times, including the Masters Tournament where he made up six shots on defending champion Palmer in the final round as Palmer slumped to a 74. This was his worst round of the tournament and pushed him down to a disappointing third place. Wall not only topped the 1959 money winners list, he was named Player of the Year and won the Vardon Trophy for the lowest stroke average.

Over the next four years the market consolidated before beginning its final leg higher in the great bull market that had begun way back in 1942 and would end at the very beginning of 1966. Over those same four years Palmer established his position as "The King". He didn't win the money title each year, missing out to Gary Player in 1961, but he did win more tournaments than any other player by far, twenty-nine in just those four seasons, including five majors – two British Opens, two Masters Tournaments and one US Open. By the end of 1963 the Dow was approaching 800 and the total prize purse on the US PGA Tour exceeded two million dollars for the first time. That year, as the market was setting new records, Palmer topped the money list with a previously unheard of amount, $128,230 – this was more than fifty percent more than any player had ever won in a single season. It was twice Bob Toski's total in 1954 and four times the sum Snead won in 1949. In an incredible echo of this the Dow at 800 was twice the level it recorded at the end of 1954 and four times its level as 1949 drew to a close.

1963 was to be the last time that "The King" would top the money list and while the Palmer era was far from over (he did have one last major in him, the 1964 Masters Tournament), a new era was beginning.

Jack Nicklaus officially turned pro in 1961 but his first full season was 1962 and that year he won his first professional title. It was a major, the 1962 US Open, beating Arnold Palmer in a playoff. That year he won two other events and finished third on the money winners list as a rookie. The following year he won five events in total, including the 1963 Masters Tournament and US PGA, and came second on the money list behind Palmer. Then in 1964, despite not winning a major, Nicklaus won his first money title thanks to four tour wins. He repeated the achievement in 1965 with five victories, including the Masters Tournament. His winnings that year were a little over $140,000, breaking Palmer's record set two years earlier of $128,230 by about ten percent. Over those two years the market had rallied more, close to twenty-five percent and total prize money had soared by an even greater amount. The peak in the Dow set in late 1965, early 1966, was set to be a high that would not be meaningfully bettered until the early 1980s. Through this period the total return of the market did continue to rise, by virtue of reinvested dividends, and so too did the money available to professional golfers, but still the ups and downs of the market were reflected in the leading money winner's take.

Having touched 1,000 in both January and February of 1966 the Dow went into a steep slide and ultimately closed the year down more than fifteen percent. A similar fall was seen in the leading money winner's total. Nicklaus had enjoyed a good year in 1965 and by many standards 1966 was an even better year. He competed in fewer tournaments, just nineteen, and won three of them, but more importantly two of them were majors. He successfully defended his Masters title and then won his first British Open title at Muirfield and so joined the elite group of players who had won all four majors, the "Grand Slam". Despite this he did not retain the money winner's title, which went to Billy Casper, who, with four wins accumulated just under $122,000 – fourteen percent less than Nicklaus had won the previous year.

From that brief, but steep, slump in the markets in 1966 the Dow rallied steadily through 1967 and 1968, once again flirting with the 1,000 level as 1968 drew to a close. The leading money winner's haul also rose, in fact it rocketed higher. In 1967 Nicklaus won five times, including one major, and topped the list with a record total of just under $190,000 and in 1968 Billy Casper once again won the title, this time with five wins and a new record total of $205,169.

As 1969 began the Dow turned its back on the seemingly impenetrable 1,000 level and started to fall in what would, over the next year and a half, turn out to be its most severe decline since the early 1940s. In 1969 the market fell, in a virtually uninterrupted fashion, by twenty percent. That year the leading money winner was Frank Beard with a total of $164,707 a fall from Billy Casper's record the year before of exactly the same percentage as the market fell. The market's decline continued through the first half of 1970, and was briefly down more than thirty-five percent – it then bottomed and recovered through the balance of the year finishing 1970 virtually where it had started. That year's money winner, Lee Trevino won almost exactly the same amount as Frank Beard had the year before – $157,037.

In addition to being a tough year in the markets, and for the leading money winner, 1970 had been Nicklaus' worst year as a professional, at least as far as where he stood on the money winnings table. In 1970 he finished fourth, but he did win four tournaments including one major, his second British Open at the home of golf, St Andrews. The Nicklaus era was well and truly established – in his first nine years as a professional he had won thirty-three tournaments, eight of them majors, topped the money list three times, never been out of the top four on the money list and been named Player of the Year once. Over the next two years, as the Dow once again approached, and very briefly exceeded, 1,000 the legend of Nicklaus, "The Golden Bear", was set to grow. He was leading money winner in both years, with record totals of $244,490 and $320,542. He won a total of twelve tournaments and three majors – the 1971 US PGA that secured his second Grand Slam, the 1972 Masters Tournament and the 1972 US Open. Markets peaked at the end of 1972 and then turned down in what would become, over the next two years, the worst stock market collapse since the 1930s.

1973's fall was painful at around twenty percent but the real rout came in the second half of 1974. In 1973 Nicklaus continued his winning ways of the prior two years capturing seven titles and the money title for the sixth time, and so breaking the record of five money winner's titles held by Ben Hogan. But his total, $320,542, in keeping with the market, was down a little from his 1972 record. 1973 also saw a record total prize pool available on the US PGA Tour, $8.6 million.

Stock markets, and the global economy, all suffered badly in 1974 and professional golfers shared at least some of that pain. The number of official events on tour fell and the total prize pool available for the year fell by half a million dollars. It was the first decline in this total since the 1957 slump, but then the fall was only about $25,000.

Despite the fall in total money available, Johnny Miller had a phenomenal year winning eight times and setting another record total of more than $353,000. Some perspective as to just how extraordinary a year Miller had is provided when one realises that Nicklaus was second in the money stakes in 1974 but only took home $238,178, more than a twenty-five percent fall from his own record year of 1972.

1974

1974 was a significant year for golf, the economy and for the stock market. All experienced historic reversals in fortune.

Johnny Miller may have had a great 1974, but he was one of the few. It was a miserable year for the stock market, the economy, business and for a very large percentage of the United States' population. Economist Arthur Okun, an advisor to President Lyndon Johnson in the 1960s, invented a measure that became known as the "Misery Index".

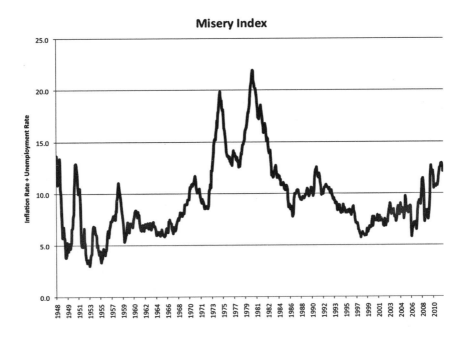

It was simply the unemployment rate added to the rate of inflation, the thinking being quite naturally that a lower rate of unemployment along with a low rate of inflation provides a constructive backdrop to the economy, whereas a high rate of unemployment and a high rate of inflation have the opposite effect, and consequently lead to misery. By this measure 1974 was as miserable as it gets.

Since 1948 the Misery Index has spent most of the time in single digits and in mid-1953, the year Ben Hogan produced one of the greatest demonstrations of consistency in the majors ever seen (winning all three that he entered), the index recorded its all time low reading of 2.97%. From there it gradually rose and by the early 1970s it had started to accelerate higher. As 1973 ended, the index stood at 13.61%, its highest reading in more than a quarter of a century, but from there things only got worse. The Misery Index rose virtually every month of 1974 before finally peaking at 19.9% in January of 1975, a record high level of misery that would only ever be surpassed, and then only marginally, during the deep recession of 1980.

The misery in the economy was more than reflected in the US stock market. Having fallen through much of 1973 it collapsed, in its worst decline since the Great Depression, in the third quarter of 1974. In the fourth quarter the market mustered something of a bounce before falling to its most depressed level since the late 1950s and down almost fifty percent from its late 1972 peak.

Amid such a gloom-laden backdrop golf was certainly not flourishing, except for Johnny Miller. The sport did still have the "Big Three" – Arnold Palmer, Jack Nicklaus and Gary Player, but collectively their heyday had passed. The Big Three brand had been launched by Mark McCormack who first agreed to manage Arnold Palmer in 1960 and then took on as his next two clients, Nicklaus and Player. From 1960 to 1966 every US Masters Tournament was won by one of the Big Three and in 1964 McCormack launched "Big Three Golf" on NBC TV. It was a powerful brand and it undoubtedly helped propel golf forward in the booming 1960s, just as the original "Great Triumvirate" of Taylor, Braid and Vardon had done six decades earlier. The power remained behind the Big Three and golf throughout the 1960s, but as the 1970s dawned and the economy and markets rolled over the Big Three seemed unable to provide the impetus required to revitalise golf.

By 1974 Arnold Palmer's last major victory was becoming a distant memory, it had been the 1964 US Masters, and he had won his sixty-second and final tour event in 1973. Gary Player won two majors in 1974, the Masters and the Open but at thirty-nine years of age there was only going to be one more major, the 1978 US Masters and only two other tour victories, also in 1978. Jack Nicklaus is four years younger than Player and ten years younger than Palmer, but by the end of 1974 Nicklaus had won close to 75% of all the tour events he was going to win and two thirds (12) of all his majors. He was still a huge power in the game and Player in 1974 had easily the best record in the majors of any golfer – two wins and a seventh and an eighth, but the Big Three were not what they had been a decade earlier.

If golf was going to recover something new was required. Howard Sounes summed up the state of professional golf in 1974 in his book *The Wicked Game*:

Total prize money for the year was $7.4 million; there was no senior tour and no second-string tour as there is now. Events were run by volunteers in an uncoordinated way and few tournaments were televised. Dwarfed by football, basketball, and baseball, golf was a minor sport in America, probably no more important than bowling, and the prospects were not auspicious. Networks were wary of investing in golf, not least because it was expensive to cover. In the mid 1970's it cost about $40,000 to film and broadcast a football game; by comparison a golf tournament could cost $300,000.

Fortunately, and maybe coincidentally, for professional golf something new did come along, only this time it wasn't a new star, as had been the case with the earlier bouts of rejuvenation that golf received. In 1974 the "something new" was an administrator – Deane Beman.

Beman became the second commissioner of the PGA Tour, succeeding Joe Dey when he retired. Beman had been a successful

Deane Beman was without doubt the right man in the right place at the right time. Golf's fortunes reversed within months of his becoming commissioner in March of 1974, and so too did the fortunes of the US stock market.

amateur golfer, wining both the British Amateur Championship in 1959 and the US Amateur title in 1960 and 1963 and turned pro in 1969. On the tour he won four times but was always a short hitter and by 1974 he was ready to move from playing to administration. He felt he could achieve more as commissioner than as a player and in that he was probably correct. His twenty years in the role oversaw several revolutions in golf that took it from the minor league role it had slipped to by the mid-1970s to arguably the most successful and lucrative professional sport in the world. He changed the model for tournament sponsorship, attaching company names to events, he launched the Players' Championship and a network of Tournament Players courses around the US, he initiated the Hogan (second) Tour, introduced pension plans for players and put in place a policy requiring all tournaments support a charity. Under his watch charitable contributions from the tour rose from under a million dollars in 1974 to more than $30 million twenty years later.

Deane Beman was without doubt the right man in the right place at the right time. Golf's fortunes reversed within months of his becoming commissioner in March of 1974, and so too did the fortunes of the US stock market.

THE MID-1970S ONWARDS

The stock market recovered dramatically from its 1974 collapse and once again the Dow approached the 1,000 level in 1976. Golf took a little longer to recover. In 1975 total money and number of events once again slipped in the wake of the longest recession since the Great Depression and while Nicklaus once again captured the money titles his totals were well short of Miller's haul in 1974. The same was true in 1976, again Nicklaus won the money title, but with a slightly reduced amount, however, the total prize pool available did start to rise again.

Over the next four years Tom Watson dominated the money list, winning larger sums each year and setting a record that would stand for five years with his $530,808 in 1980. Over that same period the Dow meandered in a fairly directionless and frustrating manner, but in 1981 the money winner seemed to reconnect with the market. Tom Kite won that year's title with $375,699, a tidy sum, but not that much more than Nicklaus had won in his best ever year nine years earlier, but then the market as measured by the Dow traversed almost exactly the same range as it had in 1972; a low of 800 and a high of 1,000.

The entire period from the mid-1960s through to the early 1980s can now be looked back upon as having been a very frustrating, range bound, very long-term bear market. It unwound the enthusiasm that had grown through the great bull market that preceded it. From the post-Great Depression and war-ravaged lows of 1942 the Dow soared, in a very steady fashion, for almost a quarter of a century. The general shape, and the year-by-year ebb and flow of both this long-term bull market and the bear market that followed were captured and reflected in the money that was available to professional golfers and the amount that the leading practitioner won, and this correlation was set to continue through the decade of the 1980s. After sixteen years of frustration and disappointment the market was about to become much more rewarding for investors and professional golf was also set to become substantially more lucrative.

The 1980s began with Tom Kite winning the money title and they ended with him winning it as well. The difference in his winning totals reflects the growth in prize money that the 1980s delivered. In 1981 Kite topped the order of merit with $375,699 and throughout the decade he was one of the most consistent money winners winning at least once in every year except 1988. His best year was 1989 when he won three times, including the Players Championship, and once again topped the money list. His winnings were a record $1,395,278, an astonishing two hundred and seventy percent more than he needed to win the title in 1981. The leading money winner's total rose steadily throughout the 1980s and the Dow did too - in fact the Dow rose like it hadn't risen for decades. There was obviously a notable hiccup in the Dow, with the crash in 1987, however that year the market still recorded a gain, and as 1989 drew to a close the highs seen prior to the 1987 crash were surpassed.

From Kite's first money title to the title he won in 1989 the market's rise was not quite as dramatic as the increase in his winnings, but it was uncannily close. From the low early in the decade to the high as 1989 ended, the Dow delivered a gain of two hundred and sixty percent compared to Kite's increase of two hundred and seventy percent.

Over both the short term of the last twenty-two years, when both markets and money-winning totals have been volatile, and over the very long term, in fact as far back as records go, the ebb and flow of the US stock market has been mirrored in the ups and downs in the fortunes of the leading professional golfers, often with an almost alarming accuracy. This close relationship between the "pulses" of the two "great games" supports the idea that there is a unique relationship between golf and investment markets, but could it all just be a reflection of the overall ebb and flow of corporate fortunes and therefore sponsorship spending that would show up in other commercial sports? This is certainly possible, in fact it is probable, greater corporate well-being would lead to higher sponsorship spending and so flow through to the professional participants. A rising tide may lift all boats, but they don't all get lifted to anything like the same extent, the relationship between the markets and other sports is nothing like as close.

WHAT ABOUT TENNIS?

It seems intuitively obvious that the markets, over the longer term, reflect the general health of the economy and presumably the healthier the economy the more money there is for corporations like Federal Express to sponsor golf. But this is where golf's relationship with the market is unique because if all that was driving golf prize money was the cause just described, then the same should be true for all sports, but it isn't.

In the late 1970s and early 1980s the most highly paid athletes in the world were tennis players and boxers. The top tennis players earned multiples of what the top golfers earned, however, in the late 2000s Roger Federer and Tiger Woods were earning comparable amounts in prize money as their respective sports leading exponents, although Tiger received far more in endorsements. It's clear that over the last few decades golfers have more than caught up with tennis players in the prize money stakes. If this is the case then golf has grown with rising markets to a far greater extent than tennis.

The difference in growth rates for leading tennis professionals compared to leading golfers can be seen in the comparison between first place money for the men's singles champion at Wimbledon compared to first place money at the British Open and how it changed over just one decade.

In 1990 Nick Faldo won his second major of the year, the British Open at St Andrews, and his fourth major overall. He played almost flawless golf over the first three rounds and eventually cruised to a five stroke victory over Mark McNulty and Payne Stewart with a final round 71. For his efforts he received the grand total of 85,000 pounds. That same year Stefan Edberg won his fourth major, and his second Wimbledon title, when he beat Boris Becker in a gripping five set final. For his efforts Edberg received almost four times the prize money Faldo received – 230,000 pounds. Over the next decade, as stock markets boomed, the dominance of tennis over golf, at least in the prize money stakes, diminished – in fact the relationship reversed.

Ten years later, in 2000 at St Andrews, when Tiger Woods won his first British Open and so became the fifth player in history to complete the modern Grand Slam, he received a cheque for half a million pounds. This was a six fold increase on Faldo's winning purse a decade earlier, but then the decade of the 1990s had been one of the best decades ever for investment markets. That same year at Wimbledon another great, Pete Sampras, was also setting records. He won his then record-breaking thirteenth grand slam singles title and his record-equalling seventh Wimbledon singles title. For this historic achievement he took home £477,000 in prize money. A tidy sum no doubt, but barely twice the amount Edberg had won ten years earlier and more importantly less than Tiger's prize for the British Open. It seems that through the 1990s the "pulse" of golf, prize money, more than kept up with the roaring stock markets, but over the same decade the "pulse" of tennis barely crept forward.

It would be interesting to review the relative growth of prize money in tennis and golf, compared to the performance of a major investment barometer, like the Dow Jones Industrial Average, over an even longer period, but unfortunately tennis has only been "open" since 1968 and so there is a limited history. Nonetheless it is fascinating to see how the growth in the prize money of the two sports has compared to the Dow's performance through each decade.

The 1990s, as discussed above, was obviously a great decade for the market and it was also the decade when golf saw its biggest improvement in prize money with the Open's first prize surpassing that of Wimbledon. In fact measured in US dollars the Open's first prize rose five fold, just a little more than the 4.2 times increase in the Dow, while Wimbledon's first prize in 2000 was only 1.7 times the 1990 prize, when measured in US dollars.

The decade of the 1980s was a good one for the market, although not as good as the 1990s and it did contain the worst stock market crash since the 1920s. Despite the crash the Dow rose three fold, which was almost the same increase in US dollars the British Open champion received – Faldo's 1990 triumph was worth $145,000 compared to Tom Watson's $59,000 when he won his third Open in 1980. While golf prize money and the markets were tripling, tennis raced ahead. Edberg's $393,000 in 1990 was more than eight times the $47,000 that Bjorn Borg received for winning his fifth Wimbledon title. Again golf was in synch with the markets whereas tennis was moving to a different beat.

This difference is most notable in the decades of the 1970s and the 2000s. Both these decades can be characterised as poor periods for the market, in fact the Dow made virtually zero progress in both, they were also decades that saw the Wimbledon prize grow at a faster rate than that of the Open. It seems that the beat or "pulse" for tennis, rather than mirroring the markets in the way golf does, may almost operate in reverse. That is, tennis seems to flourish more than golf in more difficult periods for the market and struggles to keep pace with golf when the markets are rallying.

Undoubtedly the overall wellbeing of the economy has a lot to do with the overall spend by corporations on sponsorship and so prize money. What is clear from this brief review of tennis is that despite both sports being seen historically as somewhat "privileged" they neither grow at the same rate nor do they grow at the same time. Golf has been a reflection of the other "Great Game" for a very long time; the same cannot be said of tennis.

The ebb and flow of golf's fortunes and the prize money available has not only echoed the rise and fall of investment markets broadly, with

> **It seems that the beat or "pulse" for tennis, rather than mirroring the markets in the way golf does, may almost operate in reverse. That is, tennis seems to flourish more than golf in more difficult periods for the market and struggles to keep pace with golf when the markets are rallying.**

the two activities' "pulses" seemingly in synch as far back as records go, it has also been the case that the relative performance of one country's stock market versus another has also been reflected in the comparative performance of each country's professional golfers. The next two chapters explore this phenomenon, firstly over the formative years of golf in the late 19th and early 20th centuries and then, from the 1920s onwards, after the establishment of the biennial Ryder Cup contest.

The Ryder Cup provides a regular and widely followed measure of the relative status of the professional golfers of the two dominant golfing countries and remarkably, for more than ninety years, its results have echoed the relative performance of the stock markets on either side of the Atlantic.

APPENDIX TO CHAPTER I
Leading money winners on the US PGA Tour since records began

	Money winner	Earnings ($)		Money winner	Earnings ($)
2011	Luke Donald	6,683,214	1972	Jack Nicklaus	320,542
2010	Matt Kuchar	4,910,477	1971	Jack Nicklaus	244,491
2009	Tiger Woods	10,508,163	1970	Lee Trevino	157,037
2008	Vijay Singh	6,601,094	1969	Frank Beard	164,707
2007	Tiger Woods	10,867,052	1968	Billy Casper	205,169
2006	Tiger Woods	9,941,563	1967	Jack Nicklaus	188,998
2005	Tiger Woods	10,628,024	1966	Billy Casper	121,945
2004	Vijay Singh	10,905,166	1965	Jack Nicklaus	140,752
2003	Vijay Singh	7,573,907	1964	Jack Nicklaus	113,285
2002	Tiger Woods	6,912,625	1963	Arnold Palmer	128,230
2001	Tiger Woods	5,687,777	1962	Arnold Palmer	81,448
2000	Tiger Woods	9,188321	1961	Gary Player	64,540
1999	Tiger Woods	6,616,585	1960	Arnold Palmer	75,263
1998	David Duval	2,591031	1959	Art Wall, Jr.	53,168
1997	Tiger Woods	2,066,833	1958	Arnold Palmer	42,608
1996	Tom Lehman	1,780,159	1957	Dick Mayer	65,835
1995	Greg Norman	1,654,959	1956	Ted Kroll	72,836
1994	Nick Price	1,499,927	1955	Julius Boros	63,122
1993	Nick Price	1,478,557	1954	Bob Toski	65,820
1992	Fred Couples	1,344,188	1953	Lew Worsham	34,002
1991	Corey Pavin	979,430	1952	Julius Boros	37,033
1990	Greg Norman	1,165,477	1951	Lloyd Mangrum	26,089
1989	Tom Kite	1,395,278	1950	Sam Snead	35,759
1988	Curtis Strange	1,147,644	1949	Sam Snead	31,594
1987	Curtis Strange	925,941	1948	Ben Hogan	32,112
1986	Greg Norman	653,296	1947	Jimmy Demaret	27,937
1985	Curtis Strange	542,321	1946	Ben Hogan	42,556
1984	Tom Watson	476,260	1945	Byron Nelson	63,336
1983	Hal Sutton	426,668	1944	Byron Nelson	37,968
1982	Craig Stadler	446,462	1943	No records kept	
1981	Tom Kite	375,699	1942	Ben Hogan	13,143
1980	Tom Watson	530,808	1941	Ben Hogan	18,358
1979	Tom Watson	462,636	1940	Ben Hogan	10,655
1978	Tom Watson	362,429	1939	Henry Picard	10,303
1977	Tom Watson	310,653	1938	Sam Snead	19,534
1976	Jack Nicklaus	266,439	1937	Harry Cooper	14,139
1975	Jack Nicklaus	298,149	1936	Horton Smith	7,682
1974	Johnny Miller	353,022	1935	Johnny Revolta	9,543
1973	Jack Nicklaus	308,362	1934	Paul Runyan	6,767

CHAPTER TWO
The Formative Years
and "The Championship that Changed History"

*"It was a nice slice of the century to be young in. The times were good,
the parties were frequent, the girls were pretty, the drinks were long, and the
stock market was as strong as an ox."*
Gene Sarazen recalling the 1920s before the Wall Street Crash

It is said that as long as there has been golf there have been
professional golfers, however, through the 18th and much of the 19th
century golf was primarily played by gentlemen as the handmade clubs
and balls were exceedingly expensive. The lot of professional golfers
was largely confined to the making and repairing of the gentlemen's
equipment, often fulfilling the role of green keeper, teaching and
caddying. They also attempted to supplement their own incomes
through side bets on games among themselves.

It is generally acknowledged that the first true playing
professional golfer was Allan Robertson of St Andrews. He emerged as
the top golfer in 1843 after defeating Willie Dunn Snr of Musselburgh
in a grand match over twenty rounds in just ten days. It is said that from
that point on Robertson never lost a match when money was at stake. In
addition to his playing ability Robertson was also considered the finest
maker of golf clubs and the then "feathery" golf ball with a thriving
factory in St Andrews. One of his apprentices was Old Tom Morris
who came to work for Robertson as a fourteen-year-old in 1835, but
was fired sixteen years later after Robertson caught him using the new
"guttie" ball, made of gutta percha rubber, which would soon totally
supersede the feathery. As a result Morris ended up at Prestwick where
less than ten years later the very first Open would be played.

Robertson eventually relented and began to both make and play
with the guttie and eventually, one year before his death aged forty-

four in 1859, Robertson became the first player to break 80 around St Andrews. He was buried in the grounds of St Andrews cathedral and his epitaph reads:

Allan Robertson ~ who died 1st Sept. 1859 aged 44 years old. He was greatly esteemed for his personal worth and for many years was esteemed as the champion golfer of Scotland.

It was largely as a result of Robertson's passing, and the fact that he was considered the finest player of the game throughout much of his life, that Prestwick golf club decided to hold a competition to establish who would succeed Robertson as the "Champion Golfer". That first Open was held at Prestwick on Wednesday, 17 October 1860. Initially the championship was only for professionals and the inaugural event was won by Willie Park Snr with a score of 174 for the three rounds of the twelve-hole Prestwick course, two better than Tom Morris Snr. The following year the event was thrown "open to all the world", after complaints from amateurs, and the prior year's result was reversed with Morris Snr beating Park by four strokes. The first twelve championships were held at Prestwick and on only one occasion, 1865, was neither the name Morris nor Park on top. Park won three Opens, Tom Morris Snr won four and his son, Tom Morris Jnr, also won four. The first three of Tom Morris Jnr's championships were won in succession and so he took possession of the belt that had been the prize. There being no trophy there was no championship held in 1871, but then Morris Jnr won his fourth title, two years later in 1872, after a new trophy had been made, the current claret jug. It was to be young Tom's final championship before tragically dying aged just twenty-one.

Prize money first came into the Open in the mid-1860s but for the first eleven years the first prize was just six pounds, this rose to ten pounds in 1876 and there it stayed for the next fifteen years. Until 1890 the winner had always been a Scotsman, and a professional. This all changed when Englishman and amateur John Ball saw off the might of the professionals from Musselburgh, St Andrews, Troon and Carnoustie to secure his first and only Open. He also won his second of eight British Amateur titles that year and so became the first player to hold the two most prestigious golfing titles simultaneously. Two years later another amateur Englishman, Harold Hilton won his first of two Opens and by the time the great English golfer J H Taylor won his second of five championships, in 1895, the Scottish dominance of the Open had been well and truly broken. Scotsmen won thirty-one of the first thirty-five Opens, but they were to win just eight of the next thirty-five and only two of the seventy-five after that. Nonetheless, while the Scots' dominance of the event began to wane in the late 19th century British dominance certainly did not. From those early days in 1860 through to 1920 every single championship, with only one exception, was won by an Englishman, a Scotsman or a Channel Islander (Harry Vardon with six and Ted Ray with one were both born in Jersey). The one exception was 1907 at Hoylake when Frenchman Arnaud Massey became the first European to win the event. This feat by a European was not going to be repeated until Seve Ballesteros sensationally clinched the 1979 title at Royal Lytham.

At the same time as J H Taylor was winning his second Open in succession in 1895, the inaugural US Open was about to be held. It was originally scheduled for September at Newport Country Club, Rhode Island, however, it turned out that this clashed with the then far more important America's Cup yacht race and so the first US Open was held in October. Like the early Opens it was held over thirty-six holes and completed in one day. In the first event there were ten professionals and one amateur and it was won with a score of 173 by a local player, Horace Rawlins whose prize for winning was $150, which given the then prevailing exchange rate of about five dollars to the pound, was equal to the thirty pounds that J H Taylor earned for his Open that year.

Unlike the America's Cup challenge that preceded the US Open, where the defending American Yacht, *Defender*, whitewashed the Royal Yacht Squadron's challenger *Valkyrie III*, American golfers did not fare so well. Rawlins was an Englishman who had only recently arrived in the US where he was to take up the position of club professional at

Newport Country Club, and this was to set the tone of the US Open for years to come. Prize money may have been similar on either side of the Atlantic but the fortunes of the locals were not.

The early US Opens were dominated by expatriate Scots and a few Englishmen, as not surprisingly they were better players having learnt the game in their homeland and golf was still very new in the US. This was just beginning to change at the turn of the century when the great Harry Vardon embarked on his first tour of America.

The turn of the century also marked the beginning of an important and very long-term reversal in the relative fortunes of the stock markets on either side of the Atlantic. This turning point can be clearly seen in the chart below. It shows the relative total return from investing in the UK stock market compared to the total return of the US stock market with currency movements taken into account. What it shows is that the trend through the last two decades of the 19th century was in favour of the UK market. An investor's total return from the UK market from the early 1880s through to the late 1890s was more than fifty percent greater than in the US.

This was understandable, as the 19th century was ending and at the beginning of the 20th century Great Britain was unquestionably "Great" – its Empire spread from Canada through parts of Africa,

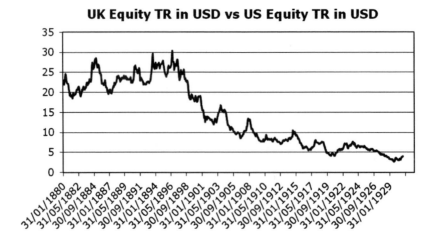

UK Equity TR in USD vs US Equity TR in USD

Bulls, Birdies, Bogeys and Bears

across India and down to Australia and New Zealand. Great Britain was the undoubted world super power. It led the world in so many areas and golf was just one of them.

Vardon's tour of the US in 1900 demonstrated in no uncertain manner that superiority, but golf was in the very early stages of a boom on that side of the Atlantic. Ten years earlier there were only a handful of golf courses in America, but by the time of Vardon's tour this number had exploded to more than a thousand with representation in every state of the union and the number of participants had increased beyond 200,000. It was a rapidly developing sport at the same time as the US was emerging as an economy and stock market of some significance.

Vardon left for the US in February 1900 as the reigning "champion golfer" having secured his third, of an eventual six, Open title at Royal St Georges in 1899. He was not yet thirty but had become the first celebrity professional golfer and was considered the finest golfer in the world. The aim of the tour was to further popularise the still young sport of golf in America and also to promote his sponsor Spalding's new ball, the Vardon Flyer. The tour was gruelling, covering over 20,000 miles and travelling as far west as Chicago with Vardon playing either a singles match against the local professional in each town visited or a match against the best ball of the two best players in a town. Vardon personally assessed his form on the tour as the best of his life. He lost only one singles match and only thirteen out of more than eighty best ball matches. He broke the tour to return to Scotland to defend his Open title at St Andrews but came second to J H Taylor. However, on his return to the US he competed in his first US Open at the Chicago Golf Club. There he got some revenge in reversing the result from St Andrews by beating Taylor by two strokes. His victory in Chicago was the first US Open to be won by a non-American based player but still the tide seemed to be against American-born golfers in their own championship. Vardon won that championship by two strokes, despite "whiffing" a one inch putt on the final hole, but his nearest American-born competitor was ten strokes back.

Over the next decade the US Open would continue to be dominated by Scottish-born players. The legendary Willie Anderson won a record-setting four of the next five and Scots won nine of the next ten, but golf in the US continued to flourish as the US economy and stock market continued to emerge.

Some evidence of this emergence of America on the golf course can be found in the amateur game on both sides of the Atlantic. While Scotsmen were dominating the professional game in America this was not quite the case among the "gentlemen" amateurs. Scottish amateurs did enjoy some early success in the US Amateur Championship, winning in 1896, 1897 and 1898, the second, third and fourth championships held. However, this run in the amateur game was to be short lived and no Scotsman was to win the event for more than the next one hundred years.

The demise of Scottish dominance of the US Amateur, and the emergence of local talent in the amateur game, was best captured in the final of the 1900 event in which Walter Travis defeated Scotsman, and 1898 champion, Finlay S Douglas who had come close to defending his title in 1899 but ultimately lost 3 and 2 in the final. After Douglas' 1900 defeat no Scotsman would appear in the final for more than thirty-five years.

Travis would go on to successfully defend his title in 1901 and to capture it again in 1903 and so became the most successful US amateur golfer in what was rapidly becoming an increasingly competitive sport in America. Travis was an American citizen; however, he was not born in America, but unlike so many of the other immigrant golfers he did learn to play in America, and at a relatively mature age.

Walter Travis was born in Australia in 1862 and didn't travel to America until 1886 when he arrived as a representative of an Australian hardware and construction products company. Four years later he married a local and soon became a naturalised American. By his late twenties he had never picked up a golf club. This would finally happen four or five years later when he was travelling in the UK and heard that his friends back home were keen to build a golf course. He bought some clubs to take back to the US and eventually started to play in his mid-thirties. He was clearly an amazing talent as within a year he had won his club championship with a then very respectable score of 82 and in little more than another year he had entered his first US Amateur. In that 1898 Championship Travis lost in the semi-final to the eventual champion, and the man he would beat in the 1900 final, Finlay S Douglas.

In his late thirties Travis, the naturalised American, was respectfully known by his competitors as the "Grand Old Man". Having learnt the game in America he had become the best amateur the country had ever produced, and he may possibly have been the best golfer, amateur or professional, that America had produced at that time. After his second Amateur title in 1901 he entered his first US Open in 1902. It was played at his home club, Garden City on Long Island. Finishing strongly with final rounds of 75 and 74 he came second to Laurie Auchterlonie who became the first player to shoot in the seventies for each round. Auchterlonie was originally from Scotland but at the time of the 1902 Open was based in Chicago. Travis' performance in the 1902 US Open would not be bettered by an American until 1911 and it remained the best performance by an amateur until 1913.

As the 20th century progressed the US stock market began to trounce the performance of the UK market and further evidence of the growing ability of American golfers, this time playing in Britain, was again provided by Walter Travis.

Five years after Vardon had won his third Open title at Royal St Georges the club hosted the 1904 British Amateur Championship and Walter Travis, by then a "Grand Old Man" of forty-two travelled to Britain for the first time to play golf. His visit began in Scotland and by all accounts his mood prior to arriving at Royal St Georges was very dark indeed. His putting, which was the back bone of his game as he was far from the longest of hitters, had deserted him. A friend suggested that the solution might be to try playing with the new Schenectady putter. This was a centre shafted putter that had been patented the year before by Arthur Franklyn Knight of Schenectady, New York.

THE DEVIL!

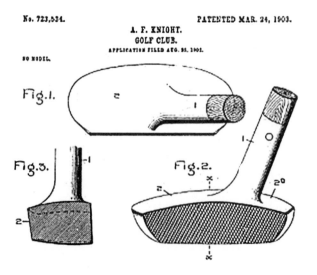

History is unclear as to how much Travis had used the new putter before arriving to compete in the British Amateur that year but the locals had never seen anything like it. For Travis it clearly cured his putting travails as he defeated former champions Horace Hutchinson and Harold Hilton on the way to the final and there beat Edward Blackwell 4 and 3. Blackwell consistently outdrove Travis by fifty yards but Travis and the Schenectady were relentless on the greens, holing putts of up to twenty yards.

Travis' victory was greeted with uproar, the trophy had never been taken out of Britain before, and many searching questions were asked as to how this could possibly have happened. Eventually it was concluded that rather than Travis being the better player it had to be the putter. Six years later the Royal and Ancient banned the Schenectady putter, and the ban endured until 1951. Throughout the years of the ban in Britain the US Golf Association continued to allow them.

Travis never returned to defend his title – in fact he never again competed in the British Amateur and so probably is the only player to have a one hundred percent record in the event – played one, won one.

With the loss of the Amateur to an American the tide in golfing fortunes was definitely turning, albeit slowly and not yet as dramatically as the relative fortunes of the two stock markets. This was to change dramatically in 1911, but first there would be another hint that a change in the long-term fortunes of the two sides of the Atlantic's golfers was imminent – the 1909 US Open.

After Travis' runner-up position in the 1902 US Open the domination by players originally from "the old country", Scotland, and England continued, but in 1909 this all appeared set to change. That year the US Open was played at Englewood Golf Club in New Jersey and over the first two rounds it appeared as if Tom McNamara, from the Wollaston Golf Club near Boston was going to rewrite history. McNamara was of Irish descent – his parents having immigrated to the US, but he was born in Brookline, Massachusetts, in 1882. In his first two rounds he shot 73 and 69, no one had ever broken 70 in the

US Open, and at the half way point McNamara was two under par and held a five stroke lead over his nearest challenger. Par had never been equalled over the four rounds of a US Open, but after such a blistering opening it seemed possible that McNamara may do so and also that an American-born golfer may finally prevail in their own open championship. In response to McNamara's opening two rounds English-born George Sargent, playing out of Hyde Manor Golf Club in Vermont, scored 72 and 71 on the final day to post the lowest score ever in the US Open, 290.

With the loss of the Amateur to an American the tide in golfing fortunes was definitely turning.

With just nine holes to play McNamara had held a three-stroke lead but suffered heat stroke on the fourteenth. After treatment he insisted on continuing but unfortunately faded to a final round 77, eventually finishing four strokes behind Sargent in second place. A locally-born golfer had come very close but still the British migrants held the upper hand in professional golf.

By the time the 1911 US Open began at the Chicago Golf Club, the scene of Vardon's victory eleven years earlier, the US market had been handsomely outperforming the UK market for several years. In fact since Vardon's victory an investor in the US market had seen their investment return more than one hundred and fifty percent while over the same period a UK investor, when measured in US dollars, had made less than ten percent. An American victory in the US Open was now long overdue.

The year before, in 1910, it again seemed that an American would win. Young American-born John McDermott, who was still only eighteen, tied with two Scottish brothers, Macdonald and Alex Smith, originally from Carnoustie. In the playoff Alex comfortably prevailed shooting 71 to secure his second US Open championship. McDermott had improved substantially since making his debut in 1909 and he continued to improve on the back of what became a legendary work ethic on the practice tee. By early 1911 his confidence was rising and he challenged local professionals to matches for the then huge sum of $1,000, but after winning three such challenges the competition dried up. It was with this rich form and confidence that McDermott arrived at Chicago. After rounds of 81, 72, 75 and 79 McDermott once again found himself in a three way tie for the title and so played off against Mike Brady, also American born, and George Simpson the next day. In the end he won with an 80 against an 82 and 85. He became the youngest ever winner of the title at just nineteen, a record that has never been bettered, but of far greater importance is that he became the first American-born golfer to win the US Open Championship – the dominance of British migrants had finally been broken.

At the 1912 US Open the ascendency of American professionals over the Scottish and English transplants became even more obvious. McDermott successfully defended his title at the Buffalo Country Club in New York with rounds of 74, 75, 74 and 71 for a two under par total of 294, the first time that par had been broken over four rounds in the US Open. American-born Tom McNamara came second and another American-born golfer, Mike Brady, tied for third with Carnoustie-born Alex Smith. The decline of British golf and the ascendency of American golf was now obvious to all. This raised more than a few concerns with a number of influential individuals back in England. They believed that something had to be done to reverse this decline and that the US Open trophy needed to be brought back to where they thought it belonged. A plan was hatched, one that would ultimately produce a totally unexpected and shocking result.

THE CHAMPIONSHIP THAT CHANGED
THE COURSE OF HISTORY

By the age of thirty-three Harry Vardon had won four British Opens and the 1900 US Open, however, his fourth Open title, the 1903 championship at Prestwick marked a turning point in his life, both from a playing and from a health perspective. After three superlative rounds of 73, 77, 72 he led his closest rivals, including his own brother, Tom, by ten strokes, this despite feeling far from well. His health deteriorated to such an extent that he considered withdrawing but he battled on and even though he shot his worst score of the week, a 78 in the final round this was still good enough to give him victory over Tom by six. After the championship he was diagnosed as suffering from tuberculosis, this curtailed his competitive golf, necessitated several stays in sanatoriums and resulted in nerve damage to the right hand that on occasions caused him serious problems with short putts. Despite these problems when his health was good he was still a match for anyone and he proved this in 1911 when he clinched his record-equalling fifth Open at Royal St Georges, the scene of his third win twelve years earlier.

After opening with consistent rounds of 74, 74 and 75, to lead Frenchman and the 1907 champion Arnaud Massey by four, it appeared that his fifth win would be at a canter. In the end it became a marathon as Vardon fell away to an 80 in the final round allowing Massey to get into a playoff after a fine 76. The following day Massey somewhat controversially conceded after thirty-five holes of the thirty-six hole playoff. Vardon's fifth Open victory, at the age of forty-one and having suffered such severe health problems was inspiring and raised his status in the minds of golf followers to an even higher level than it had ever been. It also sowed the seed of an idea in the mind of Harry's very good friend, the newspaper baron, Alfred Harmsworth, Lord Northcliffe. He proposed a repeat of the 1900 tour of the United States, partly to capitalise on Vardon's newly elevated fame, but more importantly to reassert British supremacy in golf over the rising Americans. It upset Northcliffe that the Americans were handing out defeats to

Britain in almost every sporting endeavour, be it yachting, tennis, polo or track and field. In golf he believed that supremacy still resided in Britain, although Travis' win in the 1904 Amateur Championship and McDermott's victory in the 1911 US Open were beginning to undermine this contention. Vardon agreed to tour the US in 1912 and Northcliffe set about promoting it and booked first class passage for Harry to the US. In the end Harry had to call the tour off as his health once again deteriorated and the tour was rescheduled for 1913. As it happens the liner that Harry was booked on in early 1912 was the Titanic – Harry's illness and the tour's postponement had almost certainly saved his life.

With the tour postponed Vardon's health recovered and he set about defending his Open title at Muirfield. Despite shooting a stunning 71 in the final round to make up four strokes on the leader his third round of 81 still left him in second place, four strokes behind the eventual winner – his good friend and fellow Jerseyman, Ted Ray. It was Ray's first major victory.

In the wake of Ray's victory Lord Northcliffe expanded the 1913 tour to include Ted. Ted and Harry covered almost the same distance as Harry had travelled alone twelve years earlier, only at a less leisurely pace, taking only about half the time. The culmination of the tour was to be the pair competing in the US Open at the Country Club in Brookline just outside of Boston, and if all was to go to Lord Northcliffe's plan then one of the two would avenge Travis' victory nine years earlier in the British Amateur, bring the US Open trophy back to Britain and so re-establish British superiority.

Most of the tour went according to plan with Vardon and Ray demonstrating the desired consistent and unquestionable superiority, they did not lose a match, but what was most apparent to Harry was just how much golf had progressed in America since his previous visit. Not only had the ability of the local players improved but so too had the number and the quality of the courses they played on. The level of public interest in the tour was also far greater than in 1900. Golf had clearly become an established part of the American sports scene and was growing at a dramatic pace.

Things progressed well until just prior to the US Open. Harry and Ted were entered in a stroke play event, the Shawnee Open, and the field included all the best local professionals, both British immigrants such as the Smith brothers and George Sargent and the top American-born professionals led by two-time defending US Open champion John McDermott. McDermott ran away with the event leaving Vardon, his playing partner a distant fifth and Ray an even more distant sixth.

Trans-Atlantic tensions were raised when, after the presentation, and encouraged by the crowd, the immature McDermott made some remarks to the effect that the two visiting celebrities would not be taking the US Open trophy home with them. This embarrassed members of the US Golf Association that were in attendance and resulted in McDermott being pressed into apologising, but even then he still assured the visitors that they would not win the US Open.

With tensions elevated the scene was then set for what would ultimately be remembered as the most pivotal championship in the history of the development of American golf, the 1913 US Open. What happened over the course of the championship is brilliantly described in Mark Frost's outstanding book, *The Greatest Game Ever Played* and in the movie of the same title.

Through the first two rounds of the 1913 US Open it seemed that Lord Northcliffe was going to get his wish. Vardon shot 75, 72 to lead with Ray only two strokes back after adding a 70 to his opening 79. Two further back was a young unheralded amateur playing in his first US Open, Francis Ouimet. Ouimet was a former caddy at the Country Club and lived just over the road from the course. In the third round Ouimet continued his steady play with a 74, this left him tied after three rounds with Ray and Vardon who, playing earlier had shot 76 and 78 respectively. The weather was atrocious as play continued in the afternoon and both Vardon and Ray thought they had blown their chances of victory with closing 79s but player after player faltered,

Group photo of Harry Vardon, Francis Ouimet and Edward 'Ted' Ray, c1913

until it seemed there was only one person who could thwart Lord Northcliffe's aspirations – the twenty-year-old Ouimet. When Ouimet learned of the situation he too began to falter but eventually managed to play the last six holes in two under par, impressive under any conditions let alone in the last round of the US Open in terrible weather. Those last six holes meant that Ouimet had tied with the two great Jerseymen on 304. This was three clear of four players and the previously oh so confident defending champion, McDermott, was a further stroke back. Lord Northcliffe's dream was still alive, he would have two players in the playoff the next day, but the locals' dream was also alive with their new hero, the unassuming Francis Ouimet.

The weather hadn't improved for the playoff the next day but this did little to deter the crowds. It is estimated that around 10,000 spectators followed the three players around the Brookline course that Saturday and the drama of the previous two days continued. After nine holes all three were still tied, but surprisingly it was Francis that played steadiest over the closing nine. On the tenth the two Jerseymen both three putted giving Francis a lead that would grow as the match wore on. In the end Ouimet scored his best round of the tournament in the playoff, a 72, this bettered Vardon by five and Ray by six. Francis not only ensured that the trophy stayed in America and that Lord Northcliffe left empty handed, he also became the first amateur to win the US Open title.

The next day the media went overboard and the *New York Times* modestly crowned Francis the "World's Golf Champion".

It was an extraordinary achievement, Ouimet overcame enormous adversity to even be in the championship and then to beat the best that Britain had was phenomenal, but why was it "the championship that changed history" and why was it such a watershed event?

The simplest answer to this is that the 1913 US Open confirmed the end of British domination, and not just in terms of golf. The British Empire was at its greatest in the early years of the 20th century, but, by the time this championship was played some cracks had begun to appear, nonetheless Britain was still very much "Great". From an investment perspective the early years of the 20th century also heralded a change in leadership, Britain's once undoubted superiority was beginning to be questioned and rivalled by the emergence of the United States. In the sixteen years after Francis Oiumet's historic victory an investor would have been far better rewarded investing in the new emerging leader, rather than the faltering giant that Britain had become. The return from investing in America over that period was three times the return that Britain managed to deliver. A new economic and investment leader had emerged at the same time as Britain's dominance of the fairways was fading.

The significance of the 1913 US Open was not merely that those historic events at Brookline illustrated the reversal in golfing fortunes of the two countries coincident with a reversal in economic and stock market might. It also acted as a catalyst that accelerated the reversal, at least in golfing terms, in America's favour. Ouimet's victory over the best golfers that Britain could produce caused the interest in, and enthusiasm for, golf in America to not only continue its growth, but to explode.

Prior to 1913 no American had ever won the British Open, after Ouimet's victory Americans won twelve of the next fifteen championships. Not only had the period before 1913 been characterised by British domination in the Open Championship, the dominance was largely confined to three men, the Great Triumvirate of James Braid, J H Taylor and Harry Vardon. From 1894 until 1914 they won all but five of the Championships played and on three occasions they filled the first three places. That the end of the Great Triumvirate's dominance coincided with the end of British dominance is perhaps not surprising. One writer described the period until 1914 as "the most

However, it is intriguing how often the course of history in one field intertwines with the course of history in another, and together they reflect deeper and broader trends.

romantic period in British Golf", that romantic period though, heralded by Ouimet's victory, gave way to a golden period for American golf and American prosperity.

A young professional, Walter Hagen, made his US Open Championship debut in 1913 and finished just three behind the leading trio, and he along with Gene Sarazen and the immortal Bobby Jones were to emerge at the vanguard of American golfing might.

Whether the 1913 US Open was the greatest game ever played can always be debated and comparing champions and events from one era with another is one of the charms of following golf. That it marked a watershed in golfing and investment fortunes for the opposite sides of the Atlantic is much less debatable. The 1913 US Open did mark a change in the course of history, even if it didn't actually change history itself.

There is no neat cause and effect in these observations — if Ouimet hadn't won then US golf and the US investment markets would still have done what they went on to do and the same would be true of Britain. However, it is intriguing how often the course of history in one field intertwines with the course of history in another, and together they reflect deeper and broader trends.

As American golf, both amateur and professional, continued to flourish throughout the 1910s and into the 1920s trans-Atlantic rivalries in many fields continued to grow. In golf a clear measure of the "pulse" of this rivalry was about to come into being as the 1920s began — the Ryder Cup.

APPENDIX I TO CHAPTER 2

Winners of the Open Championship 1860–1930 and their nationalities

1930	Bobby Jones (a)*	United States	1892	Harold Hilton (a)	England
1929	Walter Hagen	United States	1891	Hugh Kirkaldy	Scotland
1928	Walter Hagen	United States	1890	John Ball (a)	England
1927	Bobby Jones (a)	United States	1889	Willie Park, Jnr	Scotland
1926	Bobby Jones (a)	United States	1888	Jack Burns Scotland	
1925	Jim Barnes	England	1887	Willie Park, Jnr	Scotland
1924	Walter Hagen	United States	1886	David Brown	Scotland
1923	Arthur Havers	England	1885	Bob Martin	Scotland
1922	Walter Hagen	United States	1884	Jack Simpson	Scotland
1921	Jock Hutchison	United States	1883	Willie Fernie	Scotland
1920	George Duncan	Scotland	1882	Bob Ferguson	Scotland
1915–1919: No Championships			1881	Bob Ferguson	Scotland
1914	Harry Vardon	Jersey	1880	Bob Ferguson	Scotland
1913	John Henry Taylor	England	1879	Jamie Anderson	Scotland
1912	Ted Ray	Jersey	1878	Jamie Anderson	Scotland
1911	Harry Vardon	Jersey	1877	Jamie Anderson	Scotland
1910	James Braid	Scotland	1876	Bob Martin	Scotland
1909	John Henry Taylor	England	1875	Willie Park, Snr	Scotland
1908	James Braid	Scotland	1874	Mungo Park	Scotland
1907	Arnaud Massy	France	1873	Tom Kidd Scotland	
1906	James Braid	Scotland	1872	Tom Morris, Jnr	Scotland
1905	James Braid	Scotland	1871	No Championship	
1904	Jack White	Scotland	1870	Tom Morris, Jnr	Scotland
1903	Harry Vardon	Jersey	1869	Tom Morris, Jnr	Scotland
1902	Sandy Herd	Scotland	1868	Tom Morris, Jnr	Scotland
1901	James Braid	Scotland	1867	Tom Morris, Snr	Scotland
1900	John Henry Taylor	England	1866	Willie Park, Snr	Scotland
1899	Harry Vardon	Jersey	1865	Andrew Strath	Scotland
1898	Harry Vardon	Jersey	1864	Tom Morris, Snr	Scotland
1897	Harold Hilton (a)	England	1863	Willie Park, Snr	Scotland
1896	Harry Vardon	Jersey	1862	Tom Morris, Snr	Scotland
1895	John Henry Taylor	England	1861	Tom Morris, Snr	Scotland
1894	John Henry Taylor	England	1860	Willie Park, Snr	Scotland
1893	William Auchterlonie	Scotland			

*(a) denotes Amateur status

APPENDIX II TO CHAPTER 2

Winners of the US Open Championship 1895–1930 and their nationalities

1930	Bobby Jones (a)*	United States
1929	Bobby Jones (a)	United States
1928	Johnny Farrell	United States
1927	Tommy Armour	United States
1926	Bobby Jones (a)	United States
1925	Willie Macfarlane	Scotland
1924	Cyril Walker	England
1923	Bobby Jones (a)	United States
1922	Gene Sarazen	United States
1921	Jim Barnes	England
1920	Ted Ray	Jersey
1919	Walter Hagen	United States
1917 & 1918 No Championship		
1916	Chick Evans (a)	United States
1915	Jerome Travers (a)	United States
1914	Walter Hagen	United States
1913	Francis Ouimet (a)	United States
1912	John McDermott	United States
1911	John McDermott	United States
1910	Alex Smith	Scotland
1909	George Sargent	England
1908	Fred McLeod	Scotland
1907	Alec Ross	Scotland
1906	Alex Smith	Scotland
1905	Willie Anderson	Scotland
1904	Willie Anderson	Scotland
1903	Willie Anderson	Scotland
1902	Laurie Auchterlonie	Scotland
1901	Willie Anderson	Scotland
1900	Harry Vardon	Jersey
1899	Willie Smith	Scotland
1898	Fred Herd	Scotland
1897	Joe Lloyd	England
1896	James Foulis	Scotland
1895	Horace Rawlins	England

*(a) denotes Amateur status

APPENDIX III TO CHAPTER 2

Winners of the Amateur Championships 1885-1930 and their nationalities

1930	Bobby Jones	United States
1929	Cyril Tolley	England
1928	Philip Perkins	England
1927	William Tweddell	England
1926	Jess Sweetser	United States
1925	Robert Harris	Scotland
1924	Ernest Holderness	England
1923	Roger Wethered	England
1922	Ernest Holderness	England
1921	Willie Hunter	Scotland
1920	Cyril Tolley	England

1915 to 1919 No Championship

1914	J.L.C. Jenkins	Scotland
1913	Harold Hilton	England
1912	John Ball	England
1911	Harold Hilton	England
1910	John Ball	England
1909	Robert Maxwell	Scotland
1908	E.A. Lassen	England
1907	John Ball	England
1906	James Robb	Scotland
1905	Arthur Barry	England
1904	Walter Travis	United States
1903	Robert Maxwell	Scotland
1902	Charles Hutchings	England
1901	Harold Hilton	England
1900	Harold Hilton	England
1899	John Ball	England
1898	Freddie Tait	Scotland
1897	Jack Allan	Scotland
1896	Freddie Tait	Scotland
1895	Leslie Balfour-Melville	Scotland
1894	John Ball	England
1893	P.C. Anderson	Scotland
1892	John Ball	England
1891	Johnny Laidlay	Scotland
1890	John Ball	England
1889	Johnny Laidlay	Scotland
1888	John Ball	England
1887	Horace Hutchinson	England
1886	Horace Hutchinson	England
1885	Allan MacFie	England

APPENDIX IV TO CHAPTER 2

Winners of the US Amateur Championship 1895–1930 and their nationalities

1930	Bobby Jones	United States
1929	Harrison R. Johnston	United States
1928	Bobby Jones	United States
1927	Bobby Jones	United States
1926	George Von Elm	United States
1925	Bobby Jones	United States
1924	Bobby Jones	United States
1923	Max R. Marston	United States
1922	Jess Sweetser	United States
1921	Jesse P. Guilford	United States
1920	Chick Evans	United States
1919	S. Davidson Herron	United States
1917 & 1918 No Championship		
1916	Chick Evans	United States
1915	Robert A. Gardner	United States
1914	Francis Ouimet	United States
1913	Jerome Travers	United States
1912	Jerome Travers	United States
1911	Harold Hilton	England
1910	William C. Fownes Jr.	United States
1909	Robert A. Gardner	United States
1908	Jerome Travers	United States
1907	Jerome Travers	United States
1906	Eben Byers	United States
1905	Chandler Egan	United States
1904	Chandler Egan	United States
1903	Walter Travis	United States
1902	Louis N. James	United States
1901	Walter Travis	United States
1900	Walter Travis	United States
1899	H. M. Harriman	United States
1898	Findlay S. Douglas	Scotland
1897	H. J. Whigham	Scotland
1896	H. J. Whigham	Scotland
1895	Charles B. Macdonald	United States

CHAPTER THREE
The Ryder Cup

"I trust that the effect of this match will be to influence a cordial, friendly and peaceful feeling throughout the whole civilized world... I look upon the Royal and Ancient game as being a powerful force that influences the best things in humanity." Samuel Ryder

The Ryder Cup is now one of the most widely followed sporting events in the world, and its growth in popularity is easily explained given the incredibly tense and closely fought contests that have been witnessed over the last twenty-eight years. This has not always been the case. Upon the resumption of the series after World War II the event fairly rapidly became a one-sided affair, with the wealthy superstars of the United States regularly delivering defeat after defeat to the poorer relations from Great Britain — even the addition of players from the Republic of Ireland in the early 1970s did nothing to stop the inevitability of US supremacy. Consequently the public's interest in the event dwindled. By the mid-1970s the Ryder Cup was a shadow of the contest and spectacle that it would eventually become, or even that it had been in the years prior to World War II.

It is understandable that the wealth and prosperity of a country will have an influence upon the strength and depth of their sportsmen. This is not to say that a poor country cannot produce a global superstar, however, it is far more likely that a wealthy country will consistently produce world class athletes. This is by no means a hard and fast rule in all sports but it is interesting to observe, and central to the message of this book, that in golf the relationship has been very close and the Ryder Cup provides a rich history of this relationship. A history that almost perfectly illustrates that the relative confidence, or social mood, of each country, as reflected in its stock market, is and has been, a recurring coincident indicator of the likely success or otherwise of their professional golfers. The two "great games" are, and have long been, inextricably linked.

The history of the Ryder Cup can be broken into three distinct periods – the pre-war contests, the post-war years until the late 1970s, early 1980s, and the last twenty-eight years of very close contests. Not entirely coincidentally, and also not surprisingly, the relative performance of the two countries, or now regions, stock markets on either side of the Atlantic can also be broken into three similar periods. While it may seem reasonable that the longer-term "trend" of dominance of one side or the other in these matches should be similar to the longer-term trend of their respective stock markets, what is noteworthy is just how closely the two have been correlated over the last more than quarter of a century when the matches themselves have been so close.

THE EARLY YEARS

The Ryder Cup officially came in to being in 1927, with a trophy having been commissioned by British Seed magnate Samuel Ryder from London silver smiths Mappin and Webb at a cost of two hundred and fifty pounds (more than 12,000 pounds in 2012). However, prior to this first official event, held at the Worcester Country Club in Massachusetts, there had already been two "International Matches", the first at Gleneagles in 1921 and the second at Wentworth in 1926. Ryder had no involvement in the first but was there as a spectator at the second and that match could well have been the first official Ryder Cup, had the trophy been completed and, possibly more importantly, had the US PGA sanctioned the event. Both were fairly one-sided events won by the home, Great Britain, team.

Some may attribute the home win to the fact that the American team was not the strongest they could have fielded, yet it was a pattern that was to persist over the first four Ryder Cups. At Worcester in 1927 the home team prevailed 9½ to 2½, two years later the Cup returned to Great Britain and again the home side won, albeit in a closer contest, 7 to 5 at Moortown Golf Club in Leeds. In 1931 the US dominated at Scioto Country Club, Ohio, 9 to 3, but against a weakened Great Britain team as three of the defending team's younger stars, Henry Cotton, Percy Alliss and Aubrey Boomer, were deemed ineligible for the event as they were either non-residents of Britain, or, in Cotton's case, were planning to stay on in the US after the Ryder Cup was over.

In the wake of the 1929 stock market crash and the onset of the Great Depression protectionism raised its ugly head. In the US this took the form of the Tariff Act of 1930 or the Smoot-Hawley Tariff after the bill's two Republican sponsors, Senator Reed Smoot and Representative Willis C. Hawley. The act raised tariffs on more than 20,000 imported goods to record levels and it seemed that a similar sentiment of protectionism prevailed in the ranks of American professional golfers. They did not want any expatriate British professionals who lived and worked in America, of which at the time there were many, playing in the Ryder Cup for Great Britain, and they may also have felt threatened by Cotton's plans to stay on and play and compete in America after the event.

Cotton was still ineligible in 1933 when the event returned to Britain, this time to Southport and Ainsdale on Merseyside, but the home team once again came out on top 6½ to 5½ . The pattern of home team dominance continued in the 1935 event held at Ridgewood Country Club, New Jersey as America comfortably won 9 to 3. Over these first seven international challenges between the United States and Great Britain, the last five for the Ryder Cup, the home team had won.

The contests spanned a fourteen-year period that had seen the best of times and the worst of times, both in stock markets and economically, on both sides of the Atlantic. The 1920s belonged to the US market and economy, it soared through the roaring twenties to a far greater extent than that of Great Britain, and in the major championships Americans had begun to dominate. Yet after the crash, and into what would become known as the Great Depression, the British market held up to a far greater extent falling substantially less than the eighty-nine percent that the Dow Jones Industrial Average fell from 1929 to 1932. It is therefore understandable that the Ryder Cup reflected this "balance", but the balance was soon to be lost as America was about to demonstrate some real strength, not only on the golf course but also on the stock market.

By the time the 1937 Ryder Cup was held, again at Southport and Ainsdale, the US stock market had begun to exhibit some real strength. The Dow Jones Industrial Average had enjoyed its steadiest and most rewarding progress since the horrific lows of 1932 and 1933. Since the previous Ryder Cup in 1935 the US market had done nothing but go up, and by March of 1937 the market was fifty percent higher than it had been when the previous Cup ended. Over the same period the British market eked out only a modest gain. By the time the event started in late September 1937 the Dow was still thirty percent ahead of where it had been when the teams last met, fully three times the advance the British market had delivered.

With the benefit of hindsight it is now evident that what was occurring in the mid- to late-1930s was just the start of an enduring period of US stock market domination. It is therefore not surprising that the US team, captained by the flamboyant Walter Hagen for a sixth time, went on to achieve the first "away" win, in the end comfortably beating Great Britain 8 to 4.

While this may have been the beginning of a long period of economic and stock market domination, it was not going to be evident in Ryder Cup results for another decade as World War II intervened and it marked the end of the first period of Ryder Cup history. The results, including the two "international matches" at the start had been very close with each side winning four, and even at the level of individual matches the result was very close – Great Britain 50 to the United States 52. Only at the very end was US supremacy beginning to emerge, both in the markets and the matches. This was going to become more apparent once the series restarted, after the end of World War II, in 1947.

Year	Venue	Result
1921	Gleneagles, ("international match") Scotland	GB win 10½ - 4½
1926	Wentworth, ("international match") England	GB win 13½ - 1½
1927	Worcester CC, (first Ryder Cup) USA	US win 9½ - 2½
1929	Moortown GC, England	GB win 7 - 5
1931	Scioto CC, USA	US win 9 - 3
1933	Southport & Ainsdale, England	GB win 6½ - 5½
1935	Ridgewood CC, USA	US win 9 - 3
1937	Southport & Ainsdale, England	US win 8 - 4

THE MIDDLE YEARS, 1947-1981

The Ryder Cup resumed, somewhat to the surprise of many, with an invitation from the US PGA to host the event in Portland Oregon in November 1947.

During the war years the US Tour continued in a virtually uninterrupted fashion and, with the exception of 1943, the leading money winner title was awarded. Admittedly the money winner's titles that Byron Nelson collected in 1944 and 1945 were in War Bonds, but it showed that competitive golf was still being played at a very high level. Even those that served, such as Ben Hogan in the Army from 1942 until 1945, were able to resume their competitive careers as soon as they left the military. Hogan, having won the money title in 1942 with six wins, seemed to barely miss a beat upon his return – in 1945 he won five tournaments and then in 1946 won an outstanding thirteen tournaments and, not surprisingly, the money winners title.

None of this was true for those British professionals who had been active in competitive golf in the 1930s, life in war-ravaged and rationed Britain in 1947 was a world apart from that in the economic powerhouse that the US had become as it strode towards becoming the global super power.

This dichotomy between Britain and America was going to become more apparent over the coming years and it would manifest itself on the golf course, on the respective stock markets and in the relative valuation of the US dollar and the pound sterling.

The 1947 Ryder Cup nearly did not take place as the possibility of raising enough money to send the British team to the United States looked bleak. Fortunately, Robert Hudson, a wealthy businessman from Portland, Oregon, who was sponsoring the 1946 PGA Championship, heard about the challenges facing the Ryder Cup and stepped in to sponsor that event too. He had also sponsored the 1944 and 1945 Portland Opens, and so, with Hudson's backing, the event headed to Portland in November of 1947.

Oregon in early winter probably made the British team feel more at home and they had certainly been treated like royalty by Hudson, however, the mood in Britain at that time was nothing like that in America. Sterling was worth about twenty percent less versus the dollar than it had been when the Cup was last contested ten years earlier and although the UK stock market had recovered since the War, that recovery was nothing like that witnessed in the increasingly dominant United States. Just prior to the opening of the 1947 Ryder Cup the Dow Jones Industrial Average stood almost one hundred percent higher than it had been in early 1942, over that same period the British market had gained only half that amount. Over the prior three years the US market had risen forty percent whilst the British market had gained barely four percent. The performance of the two stock markets could hardly have been more different and the gulf that had opened between the two wartime allies was also very obvious on the golf course.

The first two foursome matches were exceptionally one-sided affairs – Captain, Henry Cotton, partnered by Arthur Lees only lasted twenty-seven holes before being beaten 10 and 9 by Ed Oliver and Lew Worsham. The second match did only slightly better with Fred Daly and Charlie Ward losing 6 and 5 to Sam Snead and Lloyd Mangrum.

The final two matches were a little closer but the result was still a one-sided 4–0 whitewash to the Americans. The next day the same trend continued as the Americans won the first seven of the eight single matches. Only Sam King's win over Herman Keiser in the final match prevented a total whitewash. The final 11–1 drubbing while humiliating was predictable. It was indicative of the increasing gap between the two nation's professional golfers that had actually been hinted at ten years earlier when the Americans won "away'" for the first time. It was also, unfortunately, indicative of a gap that was set to widen for most of the next three decades, and not only on the golf course.

Over the next thirty years, from 1947 through to 1977, the Ryder Cup became extremely one-sided. Over that thirty-year period, there were sixteen contests – the US won fourteen, there was one draw in 1969 and one solitary victory for Great Britain in 1957. Not only was the sequence of results one-sided, so too were the majority of the individual matches. This is illustrated by the fact that the US scored almost twice as many individual points over those three decades. While the US was dominating the Ryder Cup, the US stock market was dominating the British market. On a currency-adjusted basis, an investment in the US over those thirty years would have grown almost five times larger than a similar investment in Britain. And currency adjustments were an important factor in an investor's return from 1947 through to 1977 as what adjustments there were, were all devaluations of sterling against the rising dollar.

Ironically the largest of these devaluations occurred the day after the 1949 Ryder Cup ended, on the 18th September. Over the previous two days at Ganton Golf Club in Scarborough, North Yorkshire, a quite different match than that of two years earlier was played out. After the first day's foursomes the British were actually ahead, an unfamiliar position by then as they had not led after the first day since 1933, their last victorious year. Unfortunately for the British their first day momentum evaporated rapidly as Max Faulkner was beaten 8 and 7 by Ed Harrison in the top match and Charlie Ward lost 6 and 5 to Sam

Snead in the third match. America went on to dominate the singles winning all but two and so retained the trophy for a second time on British soil, but the 7 to 5 score line was a vast improvement on that of two years earlier.

That the 1949 match would be close was possibly foretold by the markets as there was little to separate the performance of the FT index and the Dow over the intervening two years. The Dow was almost exactly flat over that period and the FT had fallen about ten percent, a minor difference but the Dow was ahead and over that period there had been no changes in the relative exchange rates that were fixed at that time, however, that was about to change.

With the closing ceremony over on the Sunday evening, at 9.15pm, Sir Stafford Cripps, the Chancellor of the Exchequer, made his announcement on the BBC that the pound would be devalued by thirty percent to a new fixed exchange rate with the dollar of 2.80 dollars to the pound. Rumours had been swirling pretty much since the end of the War that such a devaluation would be necessary, but eventually it was obvious that the enormous post-war balance of payments deficit had just become too much for the country. It is intriguing that throughout the Sunday play the BBC had been making repeated announcements that the Chancellor of the Exchequer "would have something important to say at 9.15 that evening".

It is obviously highly improbable that an impending devaluation had anything to do with the British team's collapse that Sunday. Nonetheless, that devaluation was merely a continuation of the downward trend in Sterling that had been suffered since its high of more than five dollars to the pound in the early 1930s. It also made it very difficult for the UK market to give a better return than its US counterpart on a currency-adjusted basis.

Over the next two years the UK market did manage an almost thirty percent rise, which in dollar terms got it back to virtually breakeven, but over the same period, up until the next Ryder Cup in Pinehurst, North Carolina, the US market rose by more than forty percent. Reflecting a similar one-sidedness on the golf course, the Cup was very comfortably retained by America 9½ to 2½.

Over the next twenty-six years the Cup was competed for thirteen times and all Great Britain achieved was one drawn match and one lone victory. Over that same period both nations' stock markets rose about four fold to their peaks of the 1970s. Those peaks would remain all time highs for several years, but the pound continued to slide. From the 2.80 level that was established in 1949 it fell to a low point of just over 1.50 in the second half of the 1970s.

The trend of superior stock market returns for investors from the US rather than the UK was firmly established, and the dominance of the Americans in the Ryder Cup was all too clear, it is therefore more interesting to look at the two years when this seemingly established order of American dominance was turned over, or at least halted. The years were 1957, when Great Britain won for the first time in twenty-four years and after seven successive defeats, and 1969 when an unlikely and quite unexpected draw was the result.

1957

Like the first post-war Cup ten years earlier, funding was an issue for the Great Britain team in 1957 but a benefactor appeared in much the same manner as Robert Hudson had a decade earlier, this time it was a Sheffield businessman, Sir Stuart Goodwin. He agreed to gift the British PGA £10,000 to fund the event on the condition that it took place at his home course, Lindrick. And so the 1957 Ryder Cup was held at Lindrick Golf Club, Sheffield, South Yorkshire, in early October. There was some concern that the course was not long enough or that it was too similar to the type of courses that the Americans were used to, but the money had spoken and the match began amid typical autumn Yorkshire conditions. These conditions may have favoured the locals but the visitors more than rose to the challenge in the opening day's thirty-six hole foursomes matches, winning three and losing only one. Overnight it seemed that the by then inevitable rout would occur the next day. Certainly the Americans were strong favourites but despite the overwhelming tide of economic, stock market and currency supremacy streaming in the Americans favour from the late 1930s the early to mid-1950s was a period of relative calm.

Throughout the 1950s and into the 1960s the exchange rate remained fixed at 2.80 so currency movement was not a factor in calculating relative returns, all that mattered was how the respective markets fared and 1954 and 1955 were strong years for both markets. 1956 was marginally better for the US market but throughout the year both markets meandered in a fairly narrow trading range. This may have been an early indication that a closer match than had been seen for some time was in prospect but then in 1957 the UK market delivered some marked outperformance up until the week before play began. By the end of September the UK market was actually up about ten percent for the year, while the US market was down ten percent, and in the two and half months prior to the match starting the US market fell fifteen percent. It seemed the markets were foreshadowing the potential for a major upset!

This was a phenomenal performance, and an unexpected comeback that virtually no commentator would have dared to forecast, let alone have believed possible – no one that is except the stock markets of the respective countries.

On the Saturday night the prospect of a home victory seemed remote as captain Dai Rees called his players together and apparently checked score cards to determine who had, and who hadn't, played up to expectations in the disappointing foursomes series. On the basis of this examination Max Faulkner and Harry Weetman were dropped for the singles the next day, replaced by the inexperienced Peter Mills and the very experienced Harry Bradshaw. This surprising decision was more than justified the next day as the home team delivered their strongest singles performance since the 1926 forerunner of the Ryder Cup. Mills, playing at number two won his match against the American captain Jack Burke 5 and 3 and Bradshaw secured what turned out to be a redundant half against Dick Mayer playing last. All the other Great Britain players, with the exception of Peter Alliss against Fred Hawkins, won their matches — two by a margin of 7 and 6 and none were less than 4 and 3 victories. This was a phenomenal performance, and an unexpected comeback that virtually no commentator would have dared to forecast, let alone have believed possible — no one that is except the stock markets of the respective countries.

1969

From the upset in 1957 what had become normality returned for the next twelve years as American dominance accompanied yet another devaluation in sterling. In fact the one-sided nature of the contest was bringing into question the very viability of the biennial event. In the five matches after the 1957 victory the Great Britain team only managed to secure 43 points compared to the mighty Americans' 89.

If normality had returned in currency markets and Ryder Cup results, the picture in the respective country's stock markets was substantially less clear.

The great bull market that had been enjoyed on both sides of the Atlantic since 1942, only substantially more so in America, ended in the mid- to late-1960s. What followed in both countries was far greater volatility and enormous frustration on the part of investors.

In early February 1966 the Dow Jones Industrial Average flirted with 1,000 for the first time, this was an eleven fold increase from where it had been at the 1942 low. On the other hand the UK market hit its low point two years earlier, in 1940, and its high two years later in early 1969 — despite rising for four years longer it delivered only a nine fold increase in value and adjusting for the devaluations in sterling over this period, the rise was substantially less.

From 1966 onwards, for the next sixteen years the Dow swung violently around in a very broad trading range, hitting, or approaching, 1,000 half a dozen times and falling as low as 600. In the UK the market matched its high once more, in 1972, before plunging to its lowest point since the 1950s in late 1974.

As the 1969 Ryder Cup match approached, despite this volatility there were some signs from financial markets that were less negative about the UK than the US. In addition, with Tony Jacklin becoming the first "home" winner of the Open for eighteen years there was hope that the long drought of Ryder Cup success for Great Britain might end soon. Since the previous meeting in 1967 the UK market was virtually flat whereas the US market was down seventeen percent. However, there had been sterling devaluation of fourteen percent soon after the previous meeting – a devaluation that Prime Minister Harold Wilson assured the public "would not affect the pound in your pocket"! Adding all this together gave none of the clear market signals for yet another US victory as had been seen so often in the past – even though Jack Nicklaus, already a seven-time major champion, was making his long-awaited debut in the match.

The match took place at Royal Birkdale Golf Club on Merseyside and it turned out to be a thriller, nothing like the one-sided contests that so many had come to expect.

After the first day's foursomes Great Britain were ahead 4½ to 3½, the next day the scores were reversed with three of the eight matches ending in halves. So at the end of day two the match was dead level at eight points each with sixteen points in two rounds of singles matches to be played the next day.

At lunch on the final day Great Britain had edged in front and led 13 to 11 with Tony Jacklin having beaten the great Jack Nicklaus 4 and 3. This was Nicklaus' second loss in his first three rounds of Ryder Cup matches. Jacklin on the other hand was unbeaten with four wins and a half, having played in every round. On the final afternoon the overall match came down to the last two players on the course –

Nicklaus and Jacklin. Their match was all square when they reached the eighteenth tee, as was the overall match, both players found the green in two with Jacklin slightly further from the hole, his approach putt finished two feet away. Nicklaus then crouched over his twenty-five footer for the match; the putt grazed the hole but went on another five feet. He made sure of the return and before Jacklin had a chance to putt Nicklaus conceded it to him, an act of sportsmanship that captured the spirit of the Ryder Cup for years to come.

Despite this historic tie in 1969 questions continued to be asked about the Cup's credibility, especially after three more comfortable wins to the Americans in 1971, 1973, and 1975. A period that saw the US leave the gold standard, sterling start to freely trade and to fall by about a third against the dollar.

In 1973 the Great Britain team was expanded to include players from the Republic of Ireland with little effect. During another one-sided affair at Royal Lytham and St Annes in 1977 meetings took place between the two respective PGAs to discuss the future of an event that was dwindling in significance to the sporting public and players alike. It was at the 1977 Cup that Jack Nicklaus suggested including European players in the team, particularly in light of the spectacular success that one young swashbuckling Spaniard, Severiano Ballesteros, was enjoying. It was clear to everyone that something had to be done, and it was.

In 1979, the Great Britain and Ireland team was expanded to include Europeans, and two Spaniards, Seve Ballesteros and Antonio Garrido, made their debut. More Europeans would follow in 1981. At first, the inclusion of Europeans had no noticeable effect on the results with the US winning both comfortably, and in the 1979 event the two Spaniards only contributed one point out of a possible six and the overall match was lost by a by then typical 17 to 11 margin. A similar story was to unfold two years later at Walton Heath. This time Manuel Pinero and Bernhard Langer joined the team, they contributed a little more than their European predecessors two years earlier, but still the Cup was lost by a wide margin of nine points.

An observer of the stock markets of Europe and the US may not have been too surprised by these results. The US market handsomely outperformed the markets of Europe until the end of 1984, and from the end of the 1977 match to the beginning of the 1983 match, the period encompassing those first two European teams, the US market rose seventy percent while the European market measured in US dollars only rose half that amount. Despite expanding the team to be Europe, rather than just Great Britain and Ireland, the tide still seemed all in the Americans' favour. This was soon to change.

1983 ONWARDS, A TRUE CONTEST!

The seemingly inexorable decline of the Ryder Cup ended with the match at the PGA National Golf Club, Palm Beach Gardens in Florida in 1983. Tony Jacklin had been asked to take on the captaincy of the European team and he only agreed to take on the challenge if certain conditions were agreed to. He had long believed that the European teams, and before them the Great Britain and Ireland teams, always began a couple of holes down to the American superstars. The Americans always travelled in style and looked immaculate, Jacklin insisted that if he was to captain the team then they should travel first class, wear tailored rather than polyester blazers and at least be treated as equal rather than inferior to their American opponents. With all his conditions agreed to a beautifully turned out team, including for the first time three Europeans in Severiano Ballesteros, Bernhard Langer and Jose Maria Canizares, travelled to Florida on Concorde.

The match was to be very finely balanced. After the first day Europe was 4½ to 3½ ahead, this was reversed the next day so that, like in 1969, the score was even ahead of the final day singles. On the final day the lead moved around with most matches very close and another unlikely tie seeming the most probable outcome, but in the end the Americans prevailed and won by the narrowest of margins, one point.

Europe now had some true world class golfers with Langer, Ian Woosnam, Sandy Lyle and Nick Faldo all set to join Seve as major winners in the coming years. More importantly with Jacklin captaining the side they believed they could beat the Americans. The Ryder Cup was back as a true contest.

Having been such one way traffic for so long, the transformation of the Ryder Cup in 1983 was almost beyond belief, a script writer would have been ridiculed had he come up with a story line that proposed what actually happened over the next twenty-seven years. Over the previous fourteen matches America had only lost one, drawn one and won the other twelve, usually by a very wide margin. The fourteen matches from 1983 onwards saw Europe win eight, America win five and one would be drawn. But of even greater significance, both statistically and to the viewing public, has been the closeness of the majority of the matches. The 1983 14½ to 13½ score line, the closest possible deciding score would occur five more times, one match was exactly tied and two more saw the teams separated by only two points. It is no wonder that the Ryder Cup now attracts the crowds and global TV audiences that it does.

When an event becomes very one sided, or the economic and stock market fortunes of one side materially diverge from the other it is no surprise that a relationship such as the one described so far in this chapter becomes apparent. What is more surprising, and highlights the closeness of the two "great games" even better than anything else, is how the minor (and it has only been minor since 1983), ebb and flow of golfing and share market fortunes between America and Europe, over the last twenty-eight years have reflected each other.

The following chart shows the performance of the broader European stock market (including the UK), as measured by Global Financial Data in US dollars, compared to the performance of the US stock market, as measured by the S&P 500, (the return of the European market has been divided by the return of the US market) over the entire period that Europeans have been involved in the Ryder Cup.

If the line is rising then the European market is giving the better return, if it is falling then the US market is.

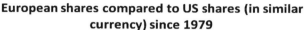

European shares compared to US shares (in similar currency) since 1979

   With just a cursory glance it is clear that the tide was running hard against the European stock market until early 1985, but then it reversed, and what a reversal it was. Over just fourteen months the European market outperformed the US market by more than eighty percent. This period included the historic events at the Belfry in September 1985 when the Europeans, now with multiple major winners in the team with Langer having won that year's Masters and Sandy Lyle having won the British Open, beat America for the first time in twenty-eight years. At the end of August, just prior to the 1985 match, the European market had delivered a twenty percent greater return than the US market since the end of the previous match. Looking at the chart it is clear that, at least from a stock market perspective, the period from early 1985 until late 1990 was strongly in favour of Europe. Then from the early 1990s, for most of the next decade, the tide shifted once again in favour of the Americans. In the early 2000s Europe was once again in the ascendency until late 2007 when the tide shifted back in favour of America.

   That "sketch" of relative market performance is also not a bad approximation of which side of the Atlantic had the upper hand in the Ryder Cup. Most European wins came when the market tide favoured Europe and similarly America tended to capture the Cup when the markets were in its favour.

While this is an interesting observation it is imprecise and it only captures "tendencies". Things get substantially more interesting when each Cup's results are studied in more detail.

After the 1985 victory confidence continued to grow among both European golfers and toward the prospects for European investment markets. Through the mid-1980s most stock markets soared and the appetite for something other than just American shares grew among global investors. As a result the US market rose by seventy-five percent prior to the 1987 Ryder Cup but the European market delivered close to a one hundred percent gain.

The 1987 Ryder Cup was to be a rematch of the two captains from 1983, Jack Nicklaus and Tony Jacklin, and it was going to be played on Jack's course, Muirfield Village. Nonetheless, it was a confident European team that boarded the Concorde, with the trophy, and flew to Columbus Ohio. The Europeans had two of the top three players in the world on the newly instituted world rankings in Seve and Langer, and with Lyle at number nine and Faldo having just secured his first British Open title there was more than a stock market tail wind behind the Europeans.

After the first two days the Europeans had built a commanding 10½ to 5½ lead, including a clean sweep in the first day's fourball matches. Only three and a half points would be needed on the last day to retain the trophy and when they finally managed to pull together three wins and three halves, for four and a half points, they had achieved something never done before, an "away" win in America, just as markets had indicated.

In 1989 the match returned to the Belfry in England's West Midlands and the Europeans were by then strong favourites to retain the trophy. Since the previous encounter Lyle had won the Masters in 1988, Seve had secured his fifth major with the 1988 British Open and Faldo had won the 1989 Masters. In late July as preparations for the match began in earnest, Europe boasted the number one, three, six, seven and eight ranked players in the world in Seve, Faldo, Ian Woosnam, Jose

Maria Olazabal and Sandy Lyle. This was probably the strongest team the Americans had ever faced in the event but despite the Europeans' confidence the one thing they lacked was the support of the markets.

Within a month of the closing ceremony of the 1987 Cup the financial world was blown apart as the worst stock market collapse since the 1929 crash shattered investor confidence. While the stock market collapse, and the surge upward that preceded it, bore a striking resemblance to the market's moves seen in the late 1920s the outcome was quite different. No depression ensued and gradually markets recovered. By the time the Ryder Cup was about to begin in 1989 both the US and the European markets had recovered back to where they had been prior to the crash. There was very little between them, but if they favoured one side it was the underdog Americans, as the US market had outperformed the European market over the preceding two years by just four percent.

Leading 9 to 7 going into the final day singles, it looked like the Europeans would continue their run of success and when they won five of the first eight matches on the final day to ensure they at least retained the trophy it looked even more certain. Amazingly the Americans won all four of the remaining matches on the course and in so doing salvaged only the second tied match in the Cup's history.

Over the next two years markets rose, then fell sharply as concerns over the possibility of war in the Middle East grew. Those fears helped drive the price of oil higher and much of the developed world faced the prospect of a recession. Coincidentally, the US market bottomed out the day the actual shooting began, and it just kept on rising. The Gulf War turned out to be fairly brief, and a success for the Americans. By the time the Ryder Cup was about to begin the US market had risen close to thirty percent from the wartime low. The European markets over the same time had only eked out a minor gain. The markets were definitely favouring the Americans ahead of the 1991 event.

With American patriotism running high after the Gulf War and the match taking place by the Atlantic, on the Ocean Course, Kiawah

Paul Runyan, USA, the first leading money winner in 1934 with less than $7,000. Playing in 1961 at Fairhaven Golf Club, Lytham *(Photo by Bob Thomas/Getty Images)*

Above: c1854. British golfers Captain Hay Wemyss
(right), 'Old' Tom Morris(left) and Allan Robertson
with his clubs under his arm (centre), at St Andrews
in Scotland. 'Old' Tom Morris and his son 'Young'
Tom became the only father and son to hold
successive Open titles when 'Old' Tom became the
oldest player to win a title, aged 46 years and 99
days, in 1867, and 'Young' Tom won in 1868. In the
following year he won again and his father finished
second. *(Photo by Hulton Archive/Getty Images)*

Right: Allan Robertson, "esteemed as the champion
golfer of Scotland".

Right: The Ryder Cup. *(Photo Getty Images)*

17th April 1929: American business man and founder of the Ryder Cup Samuel Ryder (centre) with American team captain Walter Hagen (1892 - 1969) (left) and British team captain George Duncan at a dinner function to launch the 1929 Ryder Cup at Moortown, Yorkshire.
(Photo by H. F. Davis/Topical Press Agency/Getty Images)

17th April 1929: US golfer and Ryder Cup Team captain Walter Hagen (1892 - 1969) points out various landmarks to his Ryder Cup team-mates on the roof of the Savoy Hotel, London. *(Photo by Edward G. Malindine/Topical Press Agency/Getty Images)*

Below: An unexpected victory in 1957 for the Great Britain team of -
Back Row L-R: H. Bradshaw, R.P. Mills, Peter Alliss, B.J. Hunt and H. Weetman.
Front Row L-R: M. Faulkner, E.C. Brown, captain D.J. Rees, K. Bousfield and C. O'Connor. *(Photo Getty Images)*

Above: 1969 Ryder Cup. Royal Birkdale, Lancashire. Great Britain & Ireland 16 v America 16. The Great Britain and Northern Ireland team. *(Photo Getty Images)*

'THE TEAMS THAT BATTLED TO AN HISTORIC TIE IN 1969'

Below: 1969 Ryder Cup at Royal Birkdale. A photograph of the USA team pictured standing in a line with their clubs and bags in front of them. *(Photo Getty Images)*

A fitting end to a great match as Jack Nicklaus concedes Tony Jacklin his putt for a half that ensured the overall match remained tied.

(Photo Getty Images)

Island in South Carolina, the event became known as "The War on the Shore" and America was determined to win back the trophy they had not had possession of since 1985.

On form the match may have appeared fairly even, Europe had more stars with five of the top eight players in the world but the US certainly had greater depth. After two days of foursomes and fourballs there was nothing to separate the two teams, they were locked at eight points each. As the light faded on the last day the destination of the Cup ultimately rested on the final putt on the final green.

Bernhard Langer, having fought back to all square on the final tee in his match against Hale Irwin, needed to win the last hole to secure a tie and so keep the trophy in European hands. After conceding Irwin his two foot putt for a five, Langer needed to sink his six-footer for a four and the win. At first his putt looked good, it grazed the hole but failed to fall. The Ryder Cup was back in American hands, just as the most patriotic Americans expected and the markets had suggested.

The tide of the markets had now turned in the Americans' favour and over the next couple of years the US market rose in an almost artificial manner – it just kept rising, not dramatically just very steadily. It was one of the least volatile periods ever in American market history. By the time the Cup was competed for in 1993, again at the Belfry, the markets were comfortably behind America. In the end the win for the Americans was anything but comfortable having to come from behind and achieve seven and a half points on the final day to win 15 to 13. It was their first win in Britain since 1981.

Volatility returned to markets in 1994 and 1995, and to the surprise of many it was generally good volatility in that markets rose on balance. For the first six or seven months after the 1993 Cup the European market comfortably beat its American counterpart but then in the second half of 1994 and into 1995 the American market rallied strongly and very nearly regained all it had lost since the last Ryder Cup. In the end the margin could barely have been closer but ahead of the

1995 meeting at Oak Hill Country Club in Rochester, New York, the markets were favouring the Europeans by the narrowest of margins.

In something of a reversal of the previous meeting, this time the Europeans recovered from being behind going in to the final day, they won seven and a half of the twelve points available and captured the trophy by just one point, for their second "away" win in three attempts.

1997 – THE "SPANISH" RYDER CUP

The 1997 Ryder Cup will go down in history for a number of reasons – it was the first time the event had been played on Continental Europe, it saw the debut of one Tiger Woods, it was another nail-bitingly close match and the European team that year was the first truly European team in that more of the players were European than British. But the truly historic nature of the 1997 encounter centres upon the way the form book was totally dismissed. It was the year that the "experts" and the bookmakers got the result totally wrong. It was also the only year, in the entire period from 1983 onwards, that the stock markets gave totally the wrong signal.

Going into the match both European and US markets had been rising for the preceding two years in a steady and even steepening fashion. Over that period the European market had delivered a healthy return of over twenty percent but the US had produced more than half as much again. It had been a rewarding period to be an investor, and particularly so in America.

As the teams gathered for the match at Valderrama Golf Club in Sotogrande, Spain it did appear that the holders, Europe were up against it. The match may have been at home but while some controversy surrounded the European selection process the US team virtually picked itself. Tom Kite, the US captain, described his team, as a "dream team". Six of his team were major champions and eight of his dozen were in the top thirteen in the world, the eighth ranked European ahead of the match was Italian Constantino Rocca ranked 41st in the world. In fact the US could have fielded three teams on world rankings alone and every one of those players would have been ranked higher than at least two of the European team. America has always had strength in depth, and the days of Europeans topping the world rankings had certainly faded by the time the 1997 Ryder Cup began.

If the recapturing of the Cup by a star-studded American team seemed a foregone conclusion to many, it didn't to one very important man, Severiano Ballesteros, the European captain.

Seve loved the Ryder Cup and he really loved to beat America. In many ways Seve was to golf in Europe what Arnold Palmer had been twenty years earlier to golf in America. He reignited European and British golf after decades in the doldrums and almost singlehandedly did the same for the Ryder Cup. Seve played in eight Ryder Cups and his overall record reads – 20 wins, 12 losses and 5 halved matches and as a pair, with Jose Maria Olazabal, his record was a staggering 11 wins, 2 losses and 2 halved matches.

It was Seve who played arguably the most implausible shot ever seen in the Ryder Cup in the 1983 encounter at Palm Beach. On the eighteenth, in the top singles match against Fuzzy Zoeller, Seve found his ball in a fairway bunker, close to the lip and 245 yards from the green. Throwing caution to the wind he took his 3 wood, somehow managed to clear the lip, and the ball made it to the front of the green and secured Seve a halved match. Fuzzy is reported to have said, "They say great golfers make great shots, but that one made me blink". Seve went on to make many more opponents blink in the eight Cups he competed in.

His passion for the Cup as an event and the European team was unquestionable, but over those few days in Spain in 1997 he was everywhere and undoubtedly pulled more than one-hundred percent out of all his players. They may have been the underdogs but Seve never believed that and made sure that his team didn't either. After two days the Europeans were 10½ to 5½ ahead and seemingly destined to retain the Cup but after a pep talk the night before from former US President George Bush the Americans charged back winning seven and half points out of the first eleven. This left Colin Montgomerie and Scot Hoch the only match on the course and Monty needed a half for Europe to win the Cup outright, rather than just retain it with a tied match. With phenomenally steady play up the last hole, compared to Hoch's wayward drive and missed green, Monty comfortably did this. The Cup was won by Europe, against the odds and against the markets. The deciding factor just had to be one man, Seve.

Two years later the signal from the markets was for another strong win by the Americans. Both markets surged after the 1997 Cup in spite of the crisis in Asia, but then in 1998 the phenomenal bull market that had swept the world since the early 1990s came to a shuddering halt when news broke that the huge hedge fund Long Term Capital Management (LTCM) needed bailing out. Had the bailout not been forthcoming it is difficult to imagine just what the financial and economic repercussions would have been, as it was markets suffered their most severe declines since the crash more than eleven years earlier.

> **The Cup was won by Europe, against the odds and against the markets. The deciding factor just had to be one man, Seve.**

The US market recovered very quickly and continued one of its most spectacular run-ups ever on the back of a supposed "new era" or "technological revolution". Europe rose as well, but not to the same extent as America leaving US returns comfortably ahead.

In the end the match will unfortunately be remembered for the unsporting behaviour of some elements of the American crowd and, during the closing moments of Olazabal's single match against Justin Leonard, of large parts of the American team when they invaded the 17th green after Leonard sank a crucial putt.

The final result was a one point victory to America, their first since 1993. It may not have been the easy win that the markets had forecast, but it was a win.

Shortly before the next encounter, scheduled for late September 2001, the terror attacks on the World Trade Center took place and the Ryder Cup was postponed until 2002 and the Cup henceforth became an "even" year event.

In the period between the 1999 and the 2002 event world markets haemorrhaged. The tech bubble burst and markets fell in the most severe bear market for over a quarter of a century and in a remarkable coincidence the US market bottomed less than two weeks after the 2002 Cup. In order to be consistent in assessing the forecasting ability of the markets the comparison between Europe and the US ahead of the 2002 Cup has been calculated over only the preceding two years not three. Over that period both markets fell, but, given that the speculative crescendo ahead of the 2000 peak was never as big in Europe, the European market did not fall as severely. The markets seemed to be saying that Europe would win the Cup.

In 2002 the match returned once again to the Belfry, the scene of Europe's historic 1985 win and the 1989 tie. As had happened so often in the past, the match was very close after the first two days, in fact it was dead even. The closeness continued on the final day with five of the twelve matches ending in halves, but of the remaining seven Europe won five and so won back the Cup that they had lost three years earlier.

Over the next four years markets around the world rose and memories of the devastating "Tech Wreck" and associated bear market faded, but the US was no longer the investment world's darling that it had been in the late 1990s, there were more exciting and more exotic markets for investors to explore. With the US markets being seen as somewhat boring most other markets did better, including Europe. Over this period Europe secured its two most comfortable Ryder Cup victories ever, both by a clear nine points, and so for the first time Europe had won a hat trick of Ryder Cups.

In the year after the 2006 Ryder Cup markets continued to climb what by then had become an historic bull market. Four years earlier, at the depths of the bear market in the wake of the global technology, media and telecoms bubble bursting and with the International Monetary Fund warning of the prospect of economic "stagnation", few would have dared to believe that things could become so good, so quickly. But as 2007 began the cracks in what had been a story that seemed only to get better began to show. By the end of that year the problems associated with the US sub-prime mortgage market were obvious as major banks and investment banks began writing off billions of dollars. It would be another year before the true historic reach and magnitude of these financial problems would be close to being fully appreciated but in the meantime, from late 2007 up to the start of the 2008 Ryder Cup, markets began to fall and kept falling. When the opening ceremony took place the US market had fallen about twenty percent and European markets had fallen a little more. At the same time the US dollar was rapidly being seen as a safe haven and had rallied ten percent against the euro.

When the 2008 Cup began at Valhalla Golf Club in Louisville, Kentucky, what would later become known as the GFC, the Global Financial Crisis, was in full swing. Whether the players had been reading the papers or not, and it didn't have to be just the business pages, they would have been fully aware of how grave an economic and financial situation was unfolding. The weekend ahead of the Cup Lehman Brothers, once the fourth largest investment bank in America, filed for bankruptcy, then the largest bankruptcy in US history. In the three weeks after the Cup the US market fell another twenty-six percent.

While the financial markets may have cast a shadow over events at Valhalla they were forecasting an end to European dominance of the Cup, and once again they were right. On balance both European and US markets weren't too far from where they had been at the end of the previous Ryder Cup, although in between they had risen a lot and fallen a lot. But the combined effects of the dollar strengthening in 2008 and the US not falling as much as Europe, meant that the return from the US market over the prior two years had been better than that of the European market.

The two previous Ryder Cups, with their one-sided European victories, were unusual given how close the series had become, and 2008 was unusual too, only this time it was for the magnitude of America's revenge. Their 16½ to 11½ victory was their largest winning margin since 1981.

Just as the "Tech Wreck" from 2000 to late 2002 slipped from the front of investors' minds as markets rose through the mid-2000s so too did the horrific market slide associated with the GFC. As markets rose from early 2009 the media gradually gave the preceding decline less coverage and began to focus on the rise, and it was a spectacular rise. From March 2009 through to the end of that year most markets soared between fifty percent and one hundred percent and then, through 2010 until the Ryder Cup at Celtic Manor in Wales in early October, most moved in a broad trading range. However, given markets fell sharply immediately after the previous Cup until that reversal in March of 2009 it was not obvious which market, Europe or the US, had done better in the intervening period. Added to this was the fact that the euro dollar exchange rate had been very volatile, trading in a very broad range from above 1.50 to below 1.20 dollars to the euro.

Over that period, taking currency movements into account, initially the US market did best for several months, then markets reversed and Europe dramatically outperformed the US. This was then more than made up for with a period of marked US outperformance until finally, over the last four months leading up to the Cup, Europe outperformed.

When returns are calculated up to the end of September 2010, the day prior to the start of the Cup, there is less than one tenth of one percent difference between the returns of the two markets over the intervening two years. This may have been an indication of a close match, but it gave no hint as to who would come out on top.

In the end it was a very close contest and Europe prevailed, yet again by the narrowest of margins, just one point. The markets may have indicated a close contest and it could be argued that given the relative strength Europe showed in the last few months leading up to the event, they were also hinting at a European victory.

Of the thirteen matches since 1983 one market has clearly been ahead of the other over the preceding two years on twelve occasions – only in 2010 was there no difference in performance. Of the twelve where there was an indication of which side of the Atlantic was ahead, one of those matches, 1989, ended in a tie. This leaves eleven matches where there was both a clear result and the markets had indicated a clear performance preference beforehand. Of those eleven results the market's indication was right ten times. This is an extraordinary statistic, particularly given how very close so many of those matches were.

This may all be coincidence, and I certainly would not recommend betting on the result of such closely fought contests on the back of what the respective markets have done since the previous encounter. However, this astonishing accuracy over twenty-eight years, when the matches have been so close, does support the broader observation made in this chapter that a relationship exists between the respective sides of the Atlantic's stock market performance and how they fare in the Ryder Cup. It is not the case that any kind of causal relationship exists, and having a superior stock market performance under your belt going in to the Ryder Cup in no way guarantees success, similarly a run of successful Ryder Cup campaigns does not ensure a healthy stock market. Rather, it seems that both the Ryder Cup and its outcome and the stock market generally are reflective of something far broader. They are symptoms rather than causes. They are both reflective of the overall social mood, or confidence, of each side of the Atlantic at the time and how it has grown or contracted over the prior two years.

The ebb and flow of the two "Great Games" are inextricably linked, not just in an absolute, global, sense, but on a region by region basis too.

The ebb and flow of the two "Great Games" are inextricably linked, not just in an absolute, global, sense, but on a region by region basis too.

APPENDIX TO CHAPTER 3

Measuring the actual performance of the markets from the end of the
month after the previous Cup to the beginning of the month in which
the next Cup takes place two years later, the following table summarises
this analysis. Monthly data has been used as that is all Global Financial
Data provide on Europe this far back.

Year	Best performing market	Ryder Cup result (matches ahead)
1985	Europe +20%	Europe +5
1987	Europe +20%	Europe +2
1989	US +4%	Tied
1991	US +6%	USA +1
1993	US +7%	USA +2
1995	Europe less than 1% ahead	Europe +1
1997	US +12%	Europe +1
1999	US +11%	USA +1
2002*	Europe +5%	Europe +3
2004	Europe +8%	Europe +9
2006	Europe +23%	Europe +9
2008	US +2%	USA +5
2010	Markets were even!	Europe +1

(* In the wake of September 11, 2001 terrorist attacks the Ryder Cup was postponed for a year,
moving to even rather than odd years. For the sake of this analysis, and to be consistent with all
other years only the prior two years were compared.)

CHAPTER FOUR
The Gender Gap

"Golf is a game of coordination, rhythm and grace; women have these to a high degree." Babe Didrikson Zaharias

Golf was one of the first sports in the United States to encourage female participation and competition when the Shinecock Hills Golf Club, in Southampton, Long Island, constructed a nine hole course for women and offered membership to female golfers. This was in 1891, nine years before women were allowed to compete in the Olympics. Out of the more than twelve hundred total participants in the 1900 Olympics in Paris the nineteen female competitors took part in croquet, tennis and golf.

At the outset there were some grave misgivings on the part of many male administrators as to the capability of women to complete an entire round of golf. Nonetheless, in 1895, four years after the first women were officially allowed to play golf, the US Golf Association held the inaugural Women's Amateur Championship, just one month after the first Men's Amateur Championship. Lucy Barnes Brown, not surprisingly a member of Shinecock Hills, won the tournament with an eighteen hole score of 132 over the Meadow Brook Golf Course in Hempstead, New York. A course record!

From then on the championship became a match play event and has been contested every year since with only two breaks for the First and Second World Wars. Female golf, not only in the US, has clearly flourished since then. However, it is fascinating to see how its growth has compared to that of the men's game. This comparison provides further insights into the relationship between golf and the investment markets.

WOMEN VERSUS MEN

A relatively new field of study,"socionomics", has made some interesting observations regarding the ascendance or otherwise of women in society. Socionomics is the study of the relationship between social mood and social behavior pioneered by Robert R. Prechter, Jr. Prechter explains in his book, *The Wave Principle of Human Social Behavior*, "The socionomic insight, as opposed to the conventional belief that social events determine the character of social mood, is the understanding that in fact social mood determines the character of social events."

Central to socionomic theory is that a falling social mood results in a lower stock market and a rising mood a higher stock market. In a paper on Popular Culture and the Stock Market, Robert Prechter observed that during times of falling social mood an increased number of women are elected to office and the reverse is true during periods of rising social mood. Prechter did not go on to explore whether a similar "social mood" driven effect is seen in other areas such as sport, however, a comparison of female professional golfers' earnings to their male counterparts reveals that such a socionomic relationship does appear to exist.

Professional golf for women in America began in 1944 with the formation of the Women's Professional Golf Association and the first ever US Women's Open was held in 1946. Patty Berg won the inaugural Women's US Open and collected $5,000 in prize money, at the time enormous sum – by comparison that year Lloyd Mangrum won the US Open and received only $1,500. This distortion was quickly resolved as for the next three years both champions received $2,000 and from then on the men's prize money grew far faster than the women's.

The Ladies Professional Golf Association formed in 1950 and the first "tour" was established. That year probably the most talented sports woman ever, Babe Didrikson Zaharias, topped the money winnings for the season with $14,800, and she repeated that success the following year winning more than $15,000. Through her short career (she didn't take up golf until her mid-twenties and she died aged only forty-six in 1956), she won forty-one tour events including ten majors, and in 1950 won the then "Grand Slam" of all three majors available. All this was achieved following her basket ball career and her athletics success at the 1932 Olympics where she won two gold medals and one silver medal.

From The Babe's early success the fledgling LPGA Tour continued to grow. The more than sixty years of history in women's professional golf allows a long-term comparison between the rewards available to male and female golfers and the relative success of each gender's top money winners.

The long-term history of the men's top money winner reflects both the ebb and flow of professional golfers and, in an extraordinary coincidence, the return of the stock market. Perhaps an even more noteworthy coincidence is what is revealed by comparing the top money winners from each gender all the way back to 1950.

Dow Jones Industrial Average (adjusted for inflation) compared to the ratio of the PGA / LPGA Leading Money Winners since 1950

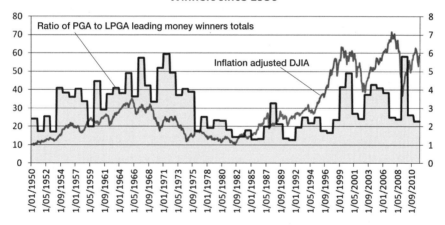

The chart (above) compares the top money winner's total from both genders each year. In 1950 The Babe's total of $14,800 is divided into Sam Snead's 1950 haul of $35,758 giving a ratio of a little over two. This is shown by the stepped line measured on the right hand scale and continues on until 2011 when Luke Donald's $6.7 million is compared to Yani Tsang's $2.9 million, again giving a ratio of a little over two. In the intervening sixty years however, this ratio has varied greatly, from close to one all the way up to six, and the swings in those ratios seem to support the socionomic contention that women achieve more through more difficult periods and amid falling social mood.

The other line on the graph is the inflation adjusted Dow Jones Industral Average over the same period and it shows that the period from 1950 through to the mid 1960s was a wonderful time to be an investor as the market rose in a virtually uninterrupted fashion. This was followed by a miserble decade and a half during which all those gains, on an inflation-adjusted basis, were given back, finally bottoming in 1982. From there the index soared through to 2000 before entering a volatile, and frustrating for investors, period of wild swings over the last twelve years.

The stepped line is an astonishing "echo" of the inflation-adjusted Dow and some of these swings warrant closer examination.

The first surge in the market from late 1953 through to 1957 marked a real acceleration in the returns investors were recieving with the Dow (not adjusted for inflation) doubling. Over that same period the most successful male golfers saw their earnings also more than double. In 1956 Ted Kroll won a then record $72,835 compared to Lew Worsham's $34,002 three years earlier, over that same period the leading female was still only winning about what The Babe won in 1950 and 1951. This trend of rising markets and greater financial success for the men versus the women continued through to the end of 1965. That year saw a record spread between the men and the women with Jack Nicklaus winning $140,752, almost five times the $29,000 that Kathy Whitworth took home. As 1965 ended the Dow was challenging 1,000 for the first time ever, it continued to threaten that level in the early weeks of the following year but then slumped in its worst fall since 1962. By October it was down close to twenty-five percent and it finally ended the year down twenty percent. With the Dow rolling over the women faired better. Kathy Whitworth was once again the leading money winner with about twenty percent more than the previous year and Jack Nicklaus was replaced by Billy Casper who won about fifteen percent less than Jack had won.

While that 1966 peak in the inflation-adjusted Dow would remain the high point for that index until well into the 1990s the high in the Dow itself was not recorded until 1972, just one year after the all time high in the ratio of gender winnings in 1971. That year, once again it was Kathy and Jack with Jack winning a staggering six times what Kathy won. But from then on it was all down hill for both investors and the men, at least when their earnings were compared to their female counterparts. Through the very challenging period of the second half of the 1970s, with inflation raging out of control, the gap narrowed dramatically. Partly this narrowing was due to the growth in the men's money winnings slowing but a far more important driver was the growth in the women's tour and what could be described as the "Nancey Lopez effect".

Nacey Lopez turned pro in 1977 and then won her first tournament in February of 1978, just one month after turning twenty-one. Through the balance of 1978 she won a further eight titles, including five in a row, and amassed a record $189,814 in winnings, this was more than four times what Kathy Whitworth had won just seven years earlier. While Tom Watson may have won a record $362,428 on the men's tour, nearly twice Lopez's total, it was only fifty percent more than Nicklaus had won in 1971. The following year Lopez continued her great form winning another eight titles and even more money, just under $200,000.

Lopez's youth, magnetism and success undoubtedly created a mini explosion of interest in women's golf. She attracted more women into the game and, importantly for the professional sport, attracted sponsors into women's golf. Despite the difficult economic times, on the back of the Lopez effect women's golf moved from being a minor to a major sport and began to challenge the men's tour.

By 1982 the US market had, in nominal terms, gone nowhere for sixteen years, and in absolute, inflation-adjusted terms, it was back where it had been thirty-two years earlier, at the dawn of the LPGA Tour in 1950. On the golf course the gap between men and women had also continued to shrink. By the end of 1982, when Craig Stadler topped the male money winners with $446,462 and JoAnne Carner topped the women's list with $310,400, the gap was as small as it had ever been.

It may have appeared that equality was looming but the market backdrop, and eventually the economic environment too, was about to change. From 1982 through to 1987 the US market rocketed higher and by 1988 this change from a depressed social mood to a far more upbeat one was becoming apparent in areas other than the stock market. In 1988 Curtis Strange became the first player to win over one million dollars in a season, this was more than three times the total Sherri Turner won on the LPGA Tour that year. Rather than approaching equality the genders had diverged dramatically. From there the market struggled and finally made a signicant low in 1990, just ahead of the Gulf War. It was in 1990 and 1991 that the two tours came closest to equality and it was amid one of the biggest investment setbacks that global markets had seen for decades. The bursting of the Japanese miracle.

1990 AND 1991

Throughout the 1980s the Japanese market had been a wonder to behold, rocketing ever higher and brushing off the effects of the 1987 crash in just a matter of a few months. By the time 1989 was drawing to a close the Nikkei Index had risen four fold over just the previous six years, but on New Year's eve the bull market ended and by October of 1990 the Japanese market had halved. That same year a Japanese golfer, Hiromi Kobayashi, for the only time ever on the LPGA Tour, was named Rookie of the Year.

The mood in late 1990 was certainly very bleak with the 1987 crash still fresh in everyone's minds, the collapse in Japan was dominating the investment media and tensions were escalating in the Middle East after Iraq's invasion of Kuwait. It wasn't only the previously high-flying Japanese stock market that was struggling, the Nikkei may have fallen by about fifty percent in the first nine months of 1990, but the US market had faltered too. By late 1990 the Dow, having finally materially surpassed the levels recorded before the crash three years earlier, and briefly flirted with 3,000 in the middle of the year, succumbed to the fears borne out by the Japanese rout and the military sabre rattling. It fell more than twenty percent in a matter of just a few weeks. The mood was certainly grim and on top of all the actual and depressing news, the bookshelves of the time were filled with doom-laden prophesies, led by the best selling hit, *The Great Depression of 1990* by Ravi Batra.

1990 was a good year for then world ranked number one Greg Norman. He didn't win any majors, although he had two top ten finishes, but he did win twice on the US tour, won the Australian Masters, won both the Vardon and Byron Nelson awards for scoring and finished top of the money winners list for the

Daniel's total in 1990 would have left her sixth on the men's money list, just ahead of the 1990 US Open champion Hale Irwin.

second time in his career. His total was $1.165 million. At the time this was the second highest amount any player had ever won in a single season, only Tom Kite a year earlier had ever won more.

Despite Norman having such a good year and amidst all the depressing economic, geopolitical and stock market news, the women were having a better one as the gender gap was narrowing dramatically.

The leading money winner on the LPGA Tour in 1990 was Beth Daniel, but she didn't just have a good year, she had a sensational year. She won seven times, including a major victory, she was named Player of the Year, she won the Vare trophy for scoring and was named the Female Athlete of the Year by the Associated Press. The rewards in prize money for such a banner year were $863,000, this was over thirty percent more than any other woman had ever won in a single year. And further illustrating the narrowing of the gender gap when it came to prize money, Daniel's total in 1990 would have left her sixth on the men's money list, just ahead of the 1990 US Open champion Hale Irwin.

The following year the mood remained bleak, but less bleak than had been the case in 1990. The Gulf War ended and with hindsight it is clear that the next Great Depression did not in fact materialise, but there was still a strong sense of caution. The Japanese market failed to recover with most of the rest of the world's markets and the gender gap continued to narrow, albeit very slightly.

Pat Bradley secured the LPGA money winner's title, she won four events, led the scoring averages, was named Player of the Year and won $763,000. This was less than Daniel had won the year before, but on the male side Corey Pavin won just $979,000. With the men's leading money winner slipping further than that of the women, the gap narrowed to its lowest degree ever, a factor of just 1.28.

1992 TO THE PRESENT

With the benefit of hindsight it is evident that the fears that so depressed the mood in 1990 and 1991 were misplaced and that for most of the developed world's stock markets (with the exception of Japan), what was suffered was merely a correction, but a correction that laid the foundation for an extremely rewarding bull market throughout the balance of the 1990s. As the markets raced higher so too did the prize money on the men's tour and the gender gap once again widened.

By 1995 the LPGA Tour had a new superstar to rival Nancey Lopez in Annika Sorenstam, and by 1997 so did the men's tour in Tiger Woods. In 1997 Woods won a little over two million dollars while Annika won $1.2 million, but by the time the bull market of the 1990s peaked in 2000 Tiger was winning over nine million dollars, almost five times what Australian Karrie Webb won that year to top the LPGA Tour's money list.

Two years later, the technology, media and telecoms bubble that had fuelled the latter stages of the 1990s' meteoric rise, had well and truly burst and through that difficult period the gap once again narrowed. That year Annika won $2.9 million while Vijay Singh won $6.9 million, the ratio that two years earlier was five times had now halved. After the depressed levels of late 2002 markets recovered and so too did the differential in favour of men until 2007 and 2008. Late 2007 saw markets peak and roll over and then continue falling throughout most of 2008 in their worst decline since the 1930s. This backdrop once again saw the rise of the women with Lorena Ochoa collecting $4.4 million in 2007 and $2.8 million in 2008, only a little under half of what Tiger won in 2007 and Vijay won in 2008.

Markets bottomed dramatically in March 2009 and then soared, and with that more favourable backdrop so too did the ratio of men's to women's winnings.

Obviously none of these turning points have been exactly coincident and importantly there is no assumption of cause or effect in this relationship that seems to have been present since professional women's golf began. However, this tendency for women's golf to fare better during more challenging times can be seen even further back in history, right back to the days of the Great Depression.

THE CURTIS CUP

Sisters Harriot and Margaret Curtis were both very early particpants in women's golf in the United States. As a thirteen-year-old, in 1897, Margaret qualified fourth in her first US Amateur and eventually went on to win that title three times, first in 1907, beating her elder sister Harriot, who was also the defending champion, in the final, and then again in 1911 and 1912.

Both sisters travelled to England in 1905 to compete in the British Ladies Amateur Championships and while they were there an informal match took place between five players from Britain and five from the US. This sowed the seed of an idea in the sisters that would eventually take twenty-seven more years to bear fruit.

Formal discussions about a regular match between the female

golfers of Britain and America finally began in 1924, however, as the economy and stock markets were booming there seemed little appetite or energy for such an event.

Probably frustrated that the male equivalent, the Walker Cup, had first taken place in 1922 the Curtis sisters donated a trophy, the Curtis Cup in 1927, inscribed with the motto "To stimulate friendly rivalry among the women golfers of many lands", but still there seemed to be no enthusiasm on the part of the governing bodies either side of the Atlantic.

It wasn't until after the stock market crash had occurred in October 1929 and with markets already having more than halved that finally, in 1931, the US Golf Association and the Ladies Golf Union of Britain agreed to co-sponsor a match. It was planned for the following year.

It really does seem that conditions do have to be tough, or the social mood depressed, for female golf to come to the fore.

May 21, 1932 is more usually associated with the successful arrival of Amelia Earhart in Ireland after the first solo trans-Atlantic flight by a woman – however, it was on that spring day at Wentworth Golf Club in Surrey that the first Curtis Cup took place. The result was a 5½ to 3½ win for the Americans, led by Marion Hollins, over Joyce Wethered's British team.

It does seem bizarre that throughout the economic and stock market boom of the 1920s there appeared to be no interest or desire to host such an event and that it wasn't until the Great Depression was in full force that it finally got off the ground. By the time the first match took place on that Saturday in May, the US market had actually fallen from a high in late August of 1929 of 383.96, to just 53.04, a catastrophic decline of eighty-six percent.

The market did have a little further to fall, but not much. By the July 8, 1932 the market finally bottomed at 40.56, down almost ninety percent over the prior thirty-five months. It really does seem that conditions do have to be tough, or the social mood depressed, for female golf to come to the fore.

THE SOLHEIM CUP

Male golfers in Britain and the US can aspire to play in the Walker Cup as amateurs and the Ryder Cup and President's Cup as professionals. For women on the other hand, for a very long time the only team event they could aim for was the Curtis Cup, and it seemed it took a Great Depression to even get that.

The First Curtis Cup match took place ten years after the first Walker Cup match, so as amateurs the women only had to wait a decade to have the same opportunity as the men. However, for professionals the story was very different. The first official Ryder Cup match was held in Massachusetts in late 1927, amidst a backdrop of booming economies and surging stock markets, but professional women golfers were going to have to wait sixty three years before a professional version of the Curtis Cup would be played. And when it finally did get off the ground the economic and investment environment was far from healthy.

Norwegian immigrant Karsten Solheim was an extraordinary innovator in the world of golf, originally an engineer for General Electric he didn't take up golf until relatively late in life, aged forty-two. Frustrated with his putter and putting he decided to create a totally new putter in his garage and in 1962 his revolutionary "Ping" putter received its first patent. Four years later what would become the world's best selling putter, the "Anser", was launched and a year after that Solheim left GE and incorporated the Karsten Manufacturing Company. From these humble beginnings one of the most influential, original and successful golf club manufacturing companies was born.

Solheim was always a major supporter of women's golf and many of the players on the LPGA Tour played Ping equipment and it was Solheim who was the driving force behind the creation of a "women's Ryder Cup". He was also the event's original sponsor and the event was named after him. Working with the LPGA Tour and the Ladies European Tour the first match was scheduled to take place in late 1990.

As preparations began for that inaugural Solheim Cup stock markets throughout most of the world were beginning to put the events of the market crash of October 1987 behind them. By the middle of 1990, with the Solheim Cup just a handful of months away, the US market had finally broken above the level it had achieved immediately before the crash and optimism was rising. In mid-July the Dow Jones Industrial Average broke through 3,000, it had risen an astonishing seventy-five percent from those "depression fear" filled lows of late October 1987. Unfortunately, with the Solheim Cup just four months away the rise in the market abruptly ended. What had been just a minor fall through the last two weeks of July became something much more severe after Iraq invaded Kuwait. Over the next couple of months, as the inaugural Solheim Cup drew nearer, the US market did nothing but slide and memories of the dark days of 1987 came flooding back. The final low of the 1990 bear market came in mid-October, with the Cup only a month away and the market down more than twenty percent.

The slide had been the worst fall since the 1987 crash, and excluding the crash it was the worst setback the market had suffered in almost a decade. While the bear market was inconsequential compared to the fall that preceded the first Curtis Cup, it was an uncanny echo of that earlier event being conceived during a boom but only coming to fruition at the depths of a decline. It is also an amazing coincidence that the same "echo" was seen when the Junior Solheim Cup was launched, for girls aged twelve to eighteen. The first junior event took place in late 2002, after more than two years of decline and just as the low point of the most severe and protracted bear market that had been suffered since the 1970s was approaching.

THE SOLHEIM CUP AS A MARKET INDICATOR?

It seems that female golf thrives when times get hard — it behaves like a contrary indicator, whereas the male game appears to be an almost perfect coincident indicator of the health of investment markets. This reversal of roles that the two games play can also be seen in the results of the Solheim Cup.

Unfortunately the Solheim Cup has a substantially shorter history than the Ryder Cup, however, the actions of the respective markets and the results of the female biennial event seem as closely correlated as those of the men's event, only in exactly the opposite manner.

Over the last eleven Ryder Cup matches where there has been both a clear winner and a clear indication from the markets (that is with either the US or European markets having performed better since the previous match), the markets have correctly forecast the result ten times. An astounding success rate of ninety-one percent. This has not been the case with the Solheim Cup.

Since the first Solheim Cup at Lake Nona in Florida in late 1990 the event has been contested every two years, however, after the 2002 match the scheduling was changed so the matches occurred on odd years so as not to clash with the rescheduled Ryder Cup. This meant that there was a match in both 2002 and 2003. In total the Solheim Cup has been competed for twelve times, the US has prevailed eight times, Europe four and there have been no ties. In fact, unlike the Ryder Cup, where more than half of the matches since 1989 have been decided by only one point or tied, the results in the Solheim Cup have tended to be more convincing with only the 2011 match ending with the teams separated by just two points.

Using the same data that produced the chart in the Ryder Cup chapter, that showed the relative performance, month by month, of the European market compared to the US market, a similar exercise to establish the predictive, or otherwise, ability of the markets over the outcome of the Solheim Cup matches can be conducted. Not surprisingly, given the contrary history of women's golf compared to the male game, the markets rather than getting the result right most of the time provide an almost perfect contrary indicator.

Ahead of the first match in 1990 the markets gave a strong signal that the Europeans would win, but the Americans won decisively by seven points. In 1992 the markets forecast an American victory, this time the Europeans prevailed by a clear four points. 1994 was a repeat of 1990, a forecasted European win turned into a convincing six point victory to the US.

1996 was the first time that the markets got it right, a US win. Over the next eleven years and six meetings of the two sides, the markets were wrong every single time. This run ended in 2009 when the markets forecast a US victory and the Americans did achieve their eighth win overall, but in 2011 the markets once again reverted to form and gave exactly the wrong signal. The US market had handily beaten the European market over the previous two years, but the European team won by two points in the closest fought match to date.

In investing an indicator that is consistently wrong is just as valuable as one that is always right, so long as the consistency is high. Over the last twenty-two years the markets and the Solheim Cup seem to pass that test. The reliability may not be quite as high as the extraordinarily high ninety-one percent that has been delivered by the markets in forecasting the Ryder Cup, but still most investors would love an indicator, even a contrary indicator, that was right eighty-three percent of the time, as has occurred with the Solheim Cup.

There undoubtedly is a "gender gap" in golf, and this gap expands and contracts over time. This ebbing and flowing, however, seems to reflect the overall condition of the investment markets. Male golf may well be a bull market sport but it seems that women, and women's golf, has come to the fore during more difficult times ever since they first played the game.

CHAPTER FIVE
America gets, and becomes, a TIGER

"The first time I ever saw Arnold Palmer, I said 'There's a star'. The first time I saw Jack Nicklaus, I said 'Superstar'. I feel the same way about Tiger Woods."
Gary Player

In the mid-1990s the US, as both an economy and to some extent as a stock market or place to invest, was beginning to regain its confidence. It had emerged out of Japan's shadows largely by not imploding when Japan had in the early years of the decade. However, the world of investing had become far more global.

Just because the era of Japan had passed, it did not automatically mean that the status of favoured investment destination would return to the US. The US may have done ok while Japan had collapsed but now there was a new game in town, the emerging markets.

Growth in Asia and much of Latin America was far more exciting than anything big old America could deliver, and the region's markets were soaring. The US was still a long way from regaining its former glory.

At the same time, America was struggling on the golf course. Having lost the Ryder Cup to Europe in 1985, the Americans, by the early 1990s, had still not regained the trophy, although it had come close with a draw in 1989. The world's number one golfers over the previous five years had been Welsh, Spanish, English and Australian. Only one American had figured at the top of the rankings and then only for a few weeks.

As the Asian boom continued, golf followed, and the number of courses and golfers in the region exploded. Golf was finally becoming a global game.

It looked like America was set to languish longer in both golfing terms as well as economically until, in the mid-1990s, something beyond the realms of coincidence or serendipity occurred. The next great world golfer emerged at exactly the same time as the next great boom in innovation and investment came about. And they were both American, (sort of).

Tiger Woods and the internet revolution broke America out of the doldrums. Tiger rapidly became the number one player in the world and the internet explosion put the US market on all investors' radar screens.

Just as the Great Triumvirate and then the Big Three propelled golf forward with greater speed, as Bernard Darwin put it all those years ago, Tiger was destined to do this a century later. The NASDAQ and the internet were going to do the same thing for the American economy and its stock market. America had emerged on both fronts. It had wished it could have been more like those emerging tigers. Now it was a "tiger" economy and a "tiger" stock market, and it had its very own Tiger on the golf course.

Incredibly, the ebb and flow of Tiger's fortunes, as he chased his ultimate goal of Jack Nicklaus' record of eighteen majors, would be an uncanny reflection of the ups and downs of the stock market during one of its most tumultuous fifteen-year periods ever.

This fifteen-year period can be broken into four distinct phases from a stock market perspective and a review of Tiger's career, with all its ups, downs and hiatuses, reveals similar highs, lows and turning points. Even more astonishingly, the first fifteen years of Jack Nicklaus's career, show a similar echo of the markets and of Tiger's progress in the pursuit of Jack's record.

Those periods, broadly speaking, are the first, second and third four years and the most recent three years.

THE FIRST FOUR YEARS

After the Gulf War-associated bear market low in October 1990 US stock markets initially rallied back quite swiftly, however, that swiftness soon gave way to what can only be described as a very gradual grind higher. At the time few complained about the lack of excitement, the crash of 1987, mini crash of 1989 and the recent bear market were all still very real in most investors' minds. Modest gains with minimal volatility were perfectly acceptable given the alternative, believed to be something far worse. This grind upwards continued through 1992, 1993 and 1994, volatility was at historic low levels and expectations for America were modest at best. These low expectations for America were largely because there was a new game in the investment world – the emerging markets, particularly those in Asia. In the six years up to the end of 1993 these Asian "Tigers", as they became known, delivered a compound annual return of more than thirty percent and in 1993 alone that return was close to one hundred percent. As the performance of Asian markets and their underlying economies became more widely known, reported and followed, investors flocked to where the action seemed to be and so America and its modest upward grind attracted less and less attention. America wanted to be more like the "Tiger" economies.

1995 continued the trend of the previous few years but gradually the rise in the markets began to accelerate a little. 1995 turned out to be the best year for investors since before the 1987 crash, the Dow Jones Industrial Average rose more than thirty percent but the NASDAQ, the index of mostly technology companies, rose more than forty percent. In years to come 1995 would be looked back upon as the start of the technological revolution and the dot com bubble. Through the first five months of 1996 the boom continued to accelerate with the Dow rising another fifteen percent and the NASDAQ another twenty percent. These were spectacular returns on top of what had already been seen over the previous twelve months and far surpassed the modest expectations born out of the earlier grind up. It seemed that America, in the form of the technology boom, had become a "Tiger" of its own.

Through June and July of 1996 much of the gains of the first five months were lost as markets suffered their most severe setback since 1990. This was to be the first of many such corrections but as each of them ended, the markets rose even faster – it was a once in a lifetime bull market. From that low point in late July/early August of 1996, over the next six months the NASDAQ soared another forty percent.

At the same time as the technology, media and telecoms boom was starting to really accelerate golf was being dragged out of the doldrums too, and by its own Tiger. Tiger Woods turned pro in August 1996 amid expectations that few, if any, sportsmen or women have ever had to deal with.

Throughout the prior twenty years the golf world had been looking for the "next Jack Nicklaus". There were many pretenders to the title from Johnny Miller, to Bobby Clampett and Hal Sutton, and at least one, Tom Watson, came close to emulating Nicklaus' achievements, but none of these golfers came close to equalling Nicklaus' haul of majors, tour wins or longevity. In young Tiger Woods there was real hope that Nicklaus' successor had arrived.

In some ways Tiger's pedigree surpassed Jack's. He had won three successive US Amateur titles in the three years before he turned pro whereas Jack "only" won two, the 1959 and 1961 titles. In 1960 Jack failed to defend his Amateur title but he did challenge, and almost win, that year's US Open, eventually coming second to Arnold Palmer with the lowest US Open score ever by an amateur.

Jack turned professional in late 1961 at a time when confidence in the US was high and the US stock market had been rising for most of the prior nineteen years. From its 1942 low to November 1961 the Dow Jones Industrial Average had risen seven fold, a massive return given that the market first achieved its 1942 level way back in the 1920s. What no one at the time knew was that this rewarding bull market still had almost five more years to run and another forty percent to rise.

There are many echoes of Jack's career throughout Tiger's to-date – and the positioning of the US stock market is only one of them. Just as Jack did, Tiger also turned professional late in what had already been a highly rewarding bull market, at the time the Dow Jones Industrial Average had risen seven fold from the depressed lows of fifteen years earlier in August 1982. Just as in Jack's career, this return was seen as remarkable as the level of the Dow in 1982 was first achieved back in 1963. And finally, just as in Jack's early career, the bull market that was running when Tiger arrived had another four years to run and would double over that period.

The period from early 1962 to early 1966 was an exceptionally benign period for investors with markets rising in a rewarding, steady, and virtually uninterrupted fashion. This was a reasonable description of the young Jack Nicklaus' first few years on tour. Jack won the US Open in 1962 along with two other titles and was named Rookie of the Year. In 1963 he won five titles, two of them majors and finished second on the money list. He won the money winner's title in both 1964 and 1965 with four wins in 1964, but no majors, and five wins including one major in 1965. By the time the stock market was peaking in late 1966 he'd won three titles, two of which were majors, finished second on the money list and secured his first Grand Slam with his British Open victory that year.

No professional golfer in history had ever announced their arrival to the world in quite such an emphatic style, and no other golfer would – that is until Tiger appeared.

While markets rose smoothly through the mid-1960s as Jack was securing his first Grand Slam they were less supportive of Tiger in his early years. Tiger's first full season was 1997 and he won his first major as a professional, that year's Masters. With that victory Tiger quashed any doubts that any observers may have had regarding what his potential might be, he didn't so much win the Masters as annihilate the rest of the field, winning from Tom Kite by twelve strokes. That year he won three more titles and topped the money list. Surprisingly, after such a dominant first full season Tiger decided to rebuild his swing, the result was that 1998 was something of a slump after his spectacular debut year, only one victory and slipping to fourth on the money list. Intriguingly 1998 was a difficult year for investors too. Even though the bull market did continue and 1998 was an up year for the markets the year contained the worst set-back markets had suffered since 1990.

In the wake of the Asian crisis that began in 1997 the huge hedge fund, Long Term Capital Management (LTCM), got into very severe difficulties and ultimately required a bailout orchestrated by the Federal Reserve. The uncertainty this spawned resulted in a twenty percent decline in the Dow Jones Industrial Average and a thirty percent fall in the then high-flying NASDAQ. After that fall however, markets rocketed higher. In the last three months of 1998 the NASDAQ rose fifty percent, easily wiping out the prior decline and the Dow rose by about half that amount.

Through 1999 and into the highs of 2000 the NASDAQ doubled and the Dow rose by another thirty percent. Tiger also got right back on the winning track.

In 1999 Tiger won an impressive eight times, including his second major, and in 2000, in a display of dominance arguably not seen since Hogan in 1953 or Jones in 1930, Tiger won nine tournaments including three majors, set a money-winning record of more than nine million dollars and secured his first Grand Slam.

1962 to 1966 was a great time for investors and was the launch pad for Jack Nicklaus' amazing career. The same was true for Tiger from 1996 through to 2000, despite the market correction in 1998. After achieving such heights in 1966 and 2000 it was always going to be difficult for markets to continue to soar and that proved to be the case. From 1966 the US stock market traded in a broad trading range for the next sixteen years, similarly, since the 2000 peak markets have once again been locked in a frustrating and volatile range.

The next few years were not going to be as kind to investors and both Jack and Tiger were to experience slumps.

THE NEXT FOUR YEARS – 1967 TO 1970 AND 2001 TO 2004

The trading range that began for the US market after the early 1966 peak would endure for sixteen years, however, there were better periods and worse periods along the way, this was also the case for Jack Nicklaus.

After the peak in 1966 markets rolled over through most of the balance of the year. In late 1966 they began to rally and 1967 was a reasonably healthy year with the Dow delivering a gain of about sixteen percent. It was another good year for Jack, he won five titles including one major and the money list, but the 1967 US Open would be the last major he would win for more than three years.

In 1968 markets meandered in a wide range and made very little headway, at the same time Jack was suffering a period of poor performance, at least by his then very high standards, some even called it a slump. He only won two events, the fewest in a year since turning pro, and neither were majors. He did finish second in both the US and British Opens but he missed the cut in the US PGA and he slipped to second on the money list.

If 1968 was disappointing for both investors and Jack then worse was to come in 1969. The Dow peaked in late 1968 at a level close to its 1966 peak but then it reversed dramatically and began its worst fall in decades. Over the next seventeen months, through to May 1970, the Dow lost thirty-five percent of its value. Through 1969 Jack only won two tournaments, again neither of them majors, and he slipped to third on the money list. In fact in the majors that year Jack delivered his worst performances since turning pro with only one top ten finish, a sixth at the British Open.

The market's plunge stopped, and dramatically reversed, in May of 1970 and the reversal was spectacular. In little more than a week the market rose fifteen percent and by the time the British Open began in late July the market had risen close to twenty percent. The year had not started well for Jack, at least not in the majors, he finished eighth in the Masters and a distant forty-ninth in the US Open but his major form undoubtedly changed with the reversal in the markets.

In a gripping finish Jack came from behind to tie a distraught Doug Sanders and then won the playoff the next day by one stroke. This broke Jack's longest major-winning drought, it had been more than three years since he secured the 1967 US Open, and he had now won all the majors at least twice, except the US PGA, but that wouldn't have to wait too long. That 1970 victory at the "Home of Golf", St Andrews, was another of the coincidences that connect Jack, Tiger and the markets over three and a half decades. The victory was Jack's second of three British Open titles and it was won at St Andrews, thirty-five years later Jack made his emotional farewell to the Open at St Andrews. That year Tiger won the event, and it was to be his second of three, to date.

2001 and 2002 were very poor years for investors. The previously high-flying NASDAQ plunged about eighty percent from its 2000 peak to its late 2002 low. This brought it back to almost exactly the same level it had been at when Tiger turned pro. On the other hand the Dow Jones Industrial Average fell substantially less, about half as much in fact. Nonetheless, the early 2000s were shaping up very poorly.

In both years Tiger won five events and in total picked up a further three majors. His victory in the 2002 US Open meant that he had won all the majors at least twice, except one, the British Open. Despite these successes Tiger's money winnings fell substantially from where they had been when the markets peaked in 2000. In both 2001 and 2002 he "only" won a little under seven million dollars, well down on his record-breaking haul in 2000 of close to ten million dollars.

In 2003, with the International Monetary Fund talking of economic "stagnation", the mood was grim among investors – nonetheless markets began to recover from their worst sell-off since the 1970s. The year was a healthy one for the Dow, but even after recovering through most of the year it still closed the year more than twelve percent below where it had peaked during Tiger's best year of 2000 and the NASDAQ still languished sixty percent below its 2000 peak. Tiger was also well below his best in 2003. Again he "only" won $6.7 million but possibly more importantly he lost the money winner's title to Vijay Singh and despite winning five times he barely figured in the majors. Only one top ten finish, fourth in the British Open, and a worst ever 39th in the US PGA.

The following year was worse for Tiger and it was little better for the markets that ended virtually where they had started and so were still well below their record highs. For Tiger, 2004, by some measures, was his worst year as a professional and comparable to 1998 when markets had plunged on the back of the LTCM collapse. In both 1998 and 2004 he only won one tournament and slipped to fourth on the money winners table. He didn't win any majors in either year but in 1998 there were three top ten finishes, in 2004 there was only one and then only just, a tie for ninth at the British Open.

After such a poor 2004 questions were being asked as to whether Tiger would come back and could he really challenge Jack's record of eighteen majors. As 2004 ended Tiger had won eight majors, but none in the past ten starts and only three top tens over that entire period. By comparison, as 1970 ended Jack had just secured his eighth major after breaking out of a similar slump. At the same time questions were being asked as to whether the worst had been seen for markets and would new highs be seen in the near future?

THE NEXT FOUR YEARS – 1971 TO 1974 AND 2005 TO 2008

2005 and 1971 were good years for both Tiger and Jack, they were also good years for the US stock market. In 2005 the market consolidated its gains of the previous couple of years and added another five percent. At the end of the year it was up about fifty percent from where it had been at the previous bear market low in late 2002. 2005 also saw Tiger's return to form, he won six tournaments, including two majors, secured his second Grand Slam and regained the money winner's title.

For Jack 1971 was remarkably similar. He won five times, including one major, the US PGA, and that victory meant that he had become the first golfer in history to win all four majors twice. He also won the money winner's title. The year also saw the US market deliver a strong performance, the Dow Jones Industrial Average rose ten percent and, like 2005 for Tiger, saw the market up about fifty percent from the previous low.

A similar pattern was seen the following year for Jack, Tiger and the markets. Both 2006 and 1972 witnessed virtually uninterrupted rises of between fifteen and twenty percent for the US market, and, in another uncanny echo across three and a half decades, both markets recorded new all time highs as the year ended.

With the backdrop of a market rising to heights not seen for six years both players recorded one of their best years ever. Jack won seven of the nineteen events he entered, including the Masters and the US Open. He also finished second in the British Open. In 2006 Tiger won eight events, two of which were majors, the British Open and the US PGA, and he came third in the Masters. Despite 2006 being so successful for Tiger it was also a year of sadness as in May he lost his father, Earl Woods. After Earl's death Tiger took a nine-week break and the effects of that absence were clear in that year's US Open as he missed the half-way cut for the first time in a major in his professional career. Coincidentally the Dow Jones Industrial Average fell close to ten percent through that absence and only resumed its upsurge two days before Tiger's return in that year's US Open.

Naturally both players were the leading money winners on tour, Jack for the fifth time and Tiger for the seventh.

1973 and 2007 were transition years for the market. In early 1973 the Dow Jones Industrial Average peaked at a fraction over 1000 amid high expectations that the rewarding run, largely driven off the back of the performance of the so called "nifty fifty" stocks, would continue. These were companies with such highly entrenched brand recognition and strong franchises, companies such as Coca Cola, Johnson and Johnson and IBM, that they had become one-decision stocks. They only had to be bought and price or valuation didn't matter. Confidence was so high that the bull market would continue that *Time Magazine*, on January 8, 1973, ran a major article under the banner headline: ***The Economy: A Gilt-Edged Year for the Stock Market***

Unfortunately the bull market, and the era of the "nifty fifty" only had days to run as that issue of *Time Magazine* hit the newsstand. 1973 was a better year for Jack Nicklaus than it was for the markets, but it wasn't as good as the previous year and it may have heralded a more difficult period for the Golden Bear. He did win seven times, but he only won one major and the following year, 1974, saw the market's decline turn in to the worst bear market since the 1920s. That year Jack endured one of his worst years as a professional. He only won two tournaments and whilst he did finish tenth or better in all that year's majors he failed to capture any of them. He also lost the top money winner's slot.

For Tiger and the markets in 2007 the transition came much later. The year began well for markets with the strength of 2006 continuing. This strength lasted until mid-July, then, as more news about problems with financial institutions and massive write-offs began to surface the market suffered a fall of more than ten percent. It was an official correction. While most of the media declared it to be nothing more than a "healthy correction" it would turn out to be the harbinger of something far more serious.

Tiger enjoyed considerable success in 2007, he would ultimately win seven times but up until that July sell-off, he had failed to add to his major haul despite two second place finishes in the Masters and the US Open. The final major of the year, the PGA, began almost exactly at the depths of the market correction and after a record-equalling 63 in the second round Tiger was always going to be difficult to catch. In the end he won his fourth PGA title and thirteenth major overall by a couple of shots from Woody Austin. Afterwards Tiger commented that even he was surprised at how much he had achieved in his career to date, and at the time there can have been few commentators who doubted that his ultimate goal of overhauling Jack's record of eighteen majors was easily within his reach – even inevitable.

Markets rallied for a couple of months after Tiger's PGA victory but then began to roll over again. Few could have conceived what was going to happen to markets over the coming years and equally few could have imagined just how Tiger's career was about to unravel.

As 2008 began markets continued to correct, but that was all it was believed to be, the true enormity of what was happening would not become apparent until the second half of the year. Tiger started well in 2008 and had a very solid performance in the Masters, ultimately finishing second to South African Trevor Immelman by three strokes. He had been so close to closing in on that fifth Masters title, just as he had been each of the prior two years when he tied for third and second.

After the 2008 Masters Tiger underwent knee surgery and took the next two months off. While he was out of the game the market recovered and then rolled over and as Tiger returned to golf for the US Open the correction was flirting with the possibility of becoming a bear market – a decline of twenty percent or more. As play at Torrey Pines in California began in mid-June the Dow Jones Industrial Average was threatening to fall below 12,000, down from

But Tiger's ultimate and extraordinary victory, rather than heralding even better times ahead would prove to be his last hurrah before a total breakdown.

more than 14,200 the previous October. The next five days were to witness some of the most astonishing golf that has ever been seen in a major championship and the playoff on the Monday would once again illustrate the indisputable connection between golf and the financial markets. But Tiger's ultimate and extraordinary victory, rather than heralding even better times ahead would prove to be his last hurrah before a total breakdown. Similarly, markets, with the Dow grimly hanging in above 12,000 and so less than a twenty percent decline, were not a sign of underlying strength – rather it was the relative calm before a financial, economic and stock market storm of historic proportions.

APPENDIX TO CHAPTER 5
Jack Nicklaus versus Tiger Woods

Years on tour		Majors won		PGA Tour events won	
Jack	Tiger	Jack	Tiger	Jack	Tiger
1962	1996	US Open (1)		3	2
1963	1997	Masters, PGA (3)	Masters (1)	8	6
1964	1998			12	7
1965	1999	Masters (4)	PGA (2)	17	15
1966	2000	Masters, The Open (6)	US Open, The Open, PGA (5)	20	24
1967	2001	US Open (7)	Masters (6)	25	29
1968	2002		Masters, US Open (8)	27	34
1969	2003			30	39
1970	2004	The Open (8)		33	40
1971	2005	PGA (9)	Masters, The Open (10)	38	46
1972	2006	Masters, US Open (11)	The Open, PGA (12)	45	54
1973	2007	PGA (12)	PGA (13)	52	61
1974	2008		US Open (14)	54	65
1975	2009	Masters, PGA (14)		59	71
1976	2010			61	
1977	2011			64	
1978	2012	The Open (15)		68	74
1979					
1980		US Open, PGA (17)		70	
1981					
1982				71	
1983					
1984				72	
1985					
1986		Masters (18)		73	

CHAPTER SIX
Golf and the Global Financial Crisis

"What we know about the Global Financial Crisis is
that we don't know very much." Paul Samuelson

The events at Torrey Pines in June 2008 will forever be remembered. There were so many breath-taking, startling and even superhuman performances that it captivated the imagination of the golfing world, and during the Monday playoff it captured the attention of an even wider audience.

At the start of the week Rocco Mediate, a forty-five-year-old professional with five tour wins over the previous seventeen years (but who had not won since 2002 and who only got into the event after a playoff for the final qualifying spot days beforehand), did not figure on anyone's radar screen as a potential champion, but then neither did one Tiger Woods.

Woods had been out of action for much of the prior two months leading up to the Open and there was some doubt as to whether he would even tee up on the opening Monday. When he did, doubt still persisted as to whether his recovering knee would last seventy two holes. In the end it had to endure substantially more than just the regulation four rounds.

After Thursday's first round Rocco was comfortably positioned at two under par, one behind the first round leaders on a difficult day when the scoring average was more than four over par. Tiger never really figured in the first day's action returning a modest one over par 72.

On Friday Tiger came to life. Having started on the tenth he stood at three over par after twenty-seven holes and facing the real prospect of missing the cut as he began the front nine at Torrey Pines. Nine holes later, and after one of the most remarkable nine holes of golf that the US Open has ever seen, Tiger was just one off the lead at two under par and he was tied with Rocco. He had shot thirty for the front nine, his back nine, one shot off the lowest nine holes ever in a US Open.

Again on Saturday Tiger played some spectacular golf on his closing nine. With his knee clearly causing him pain Tiger battled through and produced two eagles and a chip in birdie from the rough on the seventeenth to shoot a one under par seventy. This left him at three under and leading the championship by one from Englishman Lee Westwood who also shot a seventy and by two from Rocco who shot his worst score of the week, a seventy two.

Expectations for Woods were high as the final round began — on the thirteen previous occasions that he had held the 54 hole lead in a major he had always gone on to victory, but he had never before been in such pain entering a final round. As the round began, doubts as to Tiger's ability to get through the last round crept in after a double bogey on the first and then a bogey on the second. Things settled down for Tiger after that but one group ahead, much to the crowd's delight and surprise, forty-five year old Rocco was playing very solid golf.

Rocco narrowly missed birdies on the last two holes but closed with a level par seventy-one to lead in the clubhouse at one under. Out on the course the final pairing of Westwood and Woods came to the eighteenth tee both requiring birdies to tie and to force a playoff. Neither reached the par five eighteenth in two but both played on in three and were left with birdie putts. Westwood putted first from about fifteen feet. The putt was far from simple given the severe break and unfortunately he missed. This left Woods the focus of the enormous crowd's attention with what he hoped would be his final stroke of the day. After what seemed like an age Tiger stroked the twelve foot right to left breaking putt towards the hole, it appeared that the putt would slide just below the hole but it caught the side, rimmed the cup, and then fell in to an explosion from the crowd and ecstatic fist pumps and high fives from Tiger. Watching from the scorer's booth Rocco saw his chance of a certain victory snatched away from him, but there was still tomorrow.

The next day Rocco's dream of playing with the best golfer in the world, head-to-head, for the US Open would come true, and he was looking forward to it. So too were millions of golf fans all over the world, and, as it later transpired, so too were Wall Street's traders and brokers. The playoff would be on a Monday on the west coast, so Wall Street would be open for business throughout what would become an historic battle.

THE MONDAY PLAYOFF

Tiger and Rocco teed off at 9.00am in California, 12 o'clock New York time. That morning trading on the New York Stock Exchange had been unremarkable with the market slipping as it was set to do throughout the week. However, once the playoff started something unusual happened, trading volume began to fall. This became most obvious after about 2 o'clock New York time, as the players began the back nine. Through the tenth it looked like the inevitable Tiger victory march had begun, Rocco had folded, and the eighteen hole playoff was going to be as one-sided as such playoffs have tended to be in the past. Then something almost unbelievable happened. Over the next hour and a half, as the players battled from the eleventh through the fifteenth, Rocco, with three birdies and two pars, turned a three shot deficit into a one stroke advantage. It looked like history was going to be made and that Tiger would finally lose a major after having held the 54 hole lead. On the New York Stock Exchange, and throughout the investment world, it was clear that the attention of traders and investors shifted from a sliding market to the spectacle at Torrey Pines. The volume of trading fell more than thirty percent below that typically seen through early afternoon in New York. Rocco and Tiger had become the only game in town.

While it is interesting to note that overall investment activity was affected by the playoff, the effect Rocco's resurgence had on one particular share, Callaway Golf, is also highly noteworthy. Despite having had superstars like Phil Mickelson in its stable Callaway Golf's share price had been steadily declining for a year and languished at the same price it had traded at a decade earlier. Nonetheless, it was clear that the market began to recognise, as Rocco, a Callaway staff professional, appeared about to do the unthinkable through that early Monday afternoon, that a Rocco victory would be good for Callaway. Against a falling market Callaway's share price rose steadily throughout the afternoon finishing at its high for the day just as the eighteen hole playoff was about to end.

On the final green, the ninetieth hole, Rocco did have a putt to win the US Open, it was twenty feet and he narrowly missed it, by his own admission he "yanked it" slightly. That miss meant that Rocco and Tiger could not be separated over five rounds, ninety holes, under the most intense pressure and scrutiny. The playoff moved on to sudden death. By then the market was closed and with a poor tee shot by Rocco it soon became clear that there was not going to be a fairytale ending, at least not the fairytale ending that a Rocco victory would have been seen as.

Hole	1	2	3	4	5	6	7	8	9	10	11	12	13	14	15	16	17	18	Total
Par	4	4	3	4	4	4	4	3	5	4	3	4	5	4	4	3	4	5	71
Mediate	+1	+1	E	E	+1	+1	+1	+1	+2	+3	+3	+3	+2	+1	E	E	E	E	71
Woods	E	E	+1	+1	+1	E	-1	E	E	E	+1	+2	+1	+1	+1	+1	+1	E	71

The historic Monday Playoff, hole by hole, at Torrey Pines

Tiger made a steady par on the ninety-first hole and Rocco bogeyed it, with that the 2008 US Open was decided. In a way it was still a fairytale finish with a severely injured Tiger snatching victory from the jaws of defeat, not once but at least twice through the closing two rounds. It was an amazing performance from both players but maybe the most surprising aspect of the playoff was the influence it had on the New York Stock Exchange.

It is said that in 1930, when Bobby Jones returned from Britain having completed the first half of the original Grand Slam, winning the Open and Amateur championships of both Britain and America in one year, that during his ticker-tape parade volume on the New York Stock Exchange halved. That was almost certainly the most recent time golf had a meaningful influence on the market. What was even more intriguing in 2008 was how the very ebb and flow of the playoff was mirrored in Callaway's share price. The following day, as it became clear that there would be no fairytale ending for Rocco, the market once again turned its back on Callaway Golf as an investment and it slipped to yet another new low for the year.

The final and most disappointing thing, unless you're Rocco Mediate, that the 2008 US Open will be remembered for was that it would be the last time golf fans would see Tiger for many months as he announced he would be taking at least the rest of 2008 off to allow his damaged knee to recover. This was obviously a huge blow for Tiger as he pursued Jack's record and also for fans, but it was also likely that Tiger's withdrawal from competitive golf would prove an even bigger disappointment for his legion of sponsors.

In the wake of Tiger's announcement, the business TV network CNBC investigated what his absence might mean for corporate sponsors. They concluded that were Tiger to play in nine more tournaments in 2008, and win four of them then Nike would benefit to the tune of $65 to $75 million in equivalent advertising, Buick, whose name appeared on Tiger's bag, would benefit by about $5 to $10 million and Gatorade, that Tiger drank on the course, would gain about $2 million of equivalent advertising. None of these on course benefits would be there for his sponsors over the next ten months, given the magnitude of the sums involved it's easy to see why Wall Street paid so much attention to that historic playoff.

Tiger's absence from golf may have been a blow to sponsors and fans but it turned out to be only a minor distraction compared to the turmoil that was about to be seen in global financial markets. That turmoil was going to have an even greater effect upon professional golfers and their tours than Tiger's absence.

US AUTO MAKERS AND THE US TOUR

"What's good for the country is good for General Motors."

Charlie Wilson, then chairman of General Motors, made this famous statement more than fifty years ago, and for decades as both the US and GM flourished it certainly rang true. As 2008 rolled on the fortunes of the US and GM diverged, but they were both heading down.

As the 2008 US Open ended, the stock market decline that had started the previous October continued and by mid-July, as the British Open began without Tiger, the US market was down twenty-five percent. By then concerns were growing and eminent commentators such as legendary investor George Soros and former Federal Reserve Board chairman Alan Greenspan, in attempting to provide some historic perspective, described what was unfolding as the worst financial crisis since the Second World War or the worst since the Great Depression. Outside of the US some of the declines were even more severe.

The damage was particularly obvious among financial companies where write-offs totalling more than $400 billion had already been announced. Home builders and companies associated with the building and real estate industries had also suffered in the wake of the real estate bubble bursting. In addition to those companies directly affected by the global financial crisis, the share price of the once mighty General Motors was decimated. The question this raised for golfers was – what would this mean for the purses on the US PGA Tour?

One year before Charlie Wilson's famous statement *Fortune Magazine* had placed General Motors at the very top of its inaugural Fortune 500 list, it was the largest company in the world and would hold onto that title for years to come. As its fortunes grew so too did its involvement in sport sponsorship, and particularly golf. What was good for America was good for GM and so, it seemed, it was also good for golf.

They were the first automobile company to get involved in golf sponsorship when in 1958, to celebrate the company's first fifty years, they held the first Buick Open. Reflecting the company's stature the tournament offered the largest purse of any that year, $52,000, and the winner, Billy Casper, picked up a first prize cheque of $9,000. Over the years GM's involvement in golf, largely through their Buick brand, grew dramatically. Since 1984 Buick has been the official car of the PGA Tour, in addition to the Buick Open there was also the Buick Invitational and Tiger Woods was contracted as a Buick spokesman from 1999. The deal was renegotiated in 2004 for another five years with a contract reportedly worth $40 million.

As time passed it was no longer just GM among auto makers that was involved in the US Tour, as recently as 2006 eleven out of the thirty-four tournaments on the US tour had auto company title sponsors. The downturn for auto makers, particularly US auto makers, leading up to the GFC was very apparent in the sponsorship of the tour. In 2008 there were no Chrysler events, no Ford event, no Nissan event and one fewer Buick event than in 2006.

With the 2008 market plunge General Motors share price fell to below where it was when Wilson made his famous statement and was down ninety percent over the previous nine years. The once great company's total net worth was by then unchanged over more than half a century. In the world of golf, and golf prize money in particular, things had changed beyond all recognition over that period.

The year the first Buick Open was played, 1958, was also the first year total prize money on the US tour exceeded one million dollars. However, in 1954, the year GM was first named the largest company in the world, and the last time its shares were trading at the level they had fallen to by July 2008, total prize money on tour was only $600,000. This was equivalent to second place money in one of the 2008 Buick events. In 1954 the leading money winner, Bob Toski, set a then record total of just $65,000. How things had changed by the time Tiger topped the money winnings table in 2005, 2006 and 2007, each year winning around ten million dollars.

It was almost beyond belief that a company that was once an icon of corporate America could have fallen so far so fast, but as the global financial crisis continued to roll on through the second half of 2008 it was clear that golf was not immune and when the year ended the leading money winner title went to Vijay Singh with "only" $6.6 million. Still it was one hundred times greater than Bob Toski had won a little over half a century earlier, but it was down about forty percent on Tiger's winnings the previous three years and Vijay's own record year in 2004.

GOLF WAS NOT IMMUNE

With Tiger absent through the second half of 2008 interest in golf, as expected, waned. When Padraig Harrington clinched that year's PGA title after a thrilling battle with Sergio Garcia the viewing numbers were half those of the previous year when Tiger was victorious. But it wasn't just Tiger's absence that was having an effect on golf. By the time 2008 was coming to a close it had become clear that what had started as a financial crisis associated with poor lending practices in sub-prime mortgages had grown into a full blown economic crisis. The risk and fear of a lengthy global slowdown grew daily as unemployment rose throughout the world while governments and central banks seemed powerless to stop the decline despite unprecedented efforts.

The GFC was taking its toll on sponsors generally and Tiger's sponsors were balking. It was also naturally affecting the investment portfolios of professional golfers to the same extent as all other investors. As 2008 ended world stock markets had fallen in their most severe decline since the 1970s and in some cases their worst falls since the Great Depression. As 2009 began, the US market was down more than forty percent and had, a few weeks earlier, been down close to fifty percent.

Tiger Woods was, and still is, the world's highest paid sportsman, even though throughout the worst of the collapse, after the 2008 US Open, he was inactive. But, given the scale of the economic collapse that occurred, even his enormous endorsement income took a hit. As what would become known as the Great Recession wore on, the CEOs of the three US auto makers approached the US Congress, cap in hand, hoping for a $25 billion bailout. It was therefore not surprising that GM terminated their agreement with Tiger one year early. It is believed that Tiger received about $7 million a year from GM for having the Buick logo on his bag and to act as a company spokesman – the contract had been in place since 1999 and was scheduled to last another twelve months. General Motors spokespeople said that, despite the Tiger termination, the company was still committed to sponsoring both the Buick Open and Buick Invitational, apparently "indefinitely". In the end "indefinitely" came about a little sooner than expected as Buick's sponsorship of the Invitational and Open ended with the 2009 tournaments.

It was not just the PGA Tour that faced the prospect of a challenging 2009, the US LPGA Tour had already suffered a major blow as a result of the crisis. In late November the tour announced that it had "Dropped three official events from its schedule for 2009, citing the global economic crisis".

As a result of this, the total prize money available on the tour in 2009 dropped from more than $60 million to $55 million, and the futures of three unofficial season-ending events were very uncertain. The LPGA commissioner Carolyn Bivens was very clear as to what the cause of her scheduling challenges was "Like many businesses and individuals, the economic crisis we are all facing has resulted in a slightly different tournament landscape for 2009".

Even some of golf's brightest stars were affected by the rout. Bloomberg business news ran a story under the headline:

Sorenstam Loses Sleep over Investments as Golfing Career Ends

The winner of ten majors and over $22 million in prize money (more than any other woman golfer in history), was probably not after sympathy, even on the brink of retirement. However, in an interview she told reporters "I'm very involved in the stock market, I invest my money, I wish I could say wisely but I have obviously been affected. I don't think I can tell you I sleep good at night".

As 2009 began the faltering recovery in global stock markets soon wilted and by late February the US market had fallen more than fifty percent from its high. It was now the deepest stock market fall since the 1930s and questions about what top golfers were being paid were being raised regularly. Former world number one Greg Norman attracted enormous media headlines when he suggested that professional golfers should take a pay cut, he commented:

"Prize money is being scaled back in Europe, I wouldn't be surprised if prize money's scaled back in the US, just out of respect to every citizen and taxpayer over there who's suffering dramatically. It seems like on the PGA Tour the players are still playing for a million dollars first ..., like they're recession proof. I think there's got to be a lot of sensitivity shown. If I was the PGA Commissioner that's what I would be recommending."

Most people who read or heard Norman's comments would understand and possibly sympathise with his sentiments, however, they did sound like a criticism of the players but of course no player sets their own pay scale. Professional sportsmen play for whatever the market will stand and professional golfers benefited greatly from the financial boom that preceded the Great Recession, and to a much greater degree than other sports like tennis. Sponsors go wherever they feel they will get the greatest exposure and with as many dollars as they need to get that exposure. It was reasonable to think that that price was coming down in early 2009. It was also clear that sponsors and potential sponsors were becoming increasingly sensitive to the degree of scrutiny that their sponsorship spending would come under during difficult times.

Just a few days after Norman's comments hit the media the *Wall Street Journal* on February 28, ran a story titled:

NO ENTERTAINING, PLEASE – IT'S GOLF
The Outcry Over Northern Trust's Tournament Sponsorship Shows the Chill Threatening Golf and Business

The lavish client entertainment that accompanied Northern Trust's sponsorship of the Northern Trust Open at Riviera Country Club in Los Angeles attracted widespread media criticism, particularly given that Northern Trust had accepted $1.6 billion from the government's Troubled Asset Relief Programme (TARP) fund. This public outrage prompted a rapid response from Morgan Stanley, who had received $10 billion from the government, stating that while they would continue to sponsor the Memorial Tournament they would do no client entertainment at the event and Wells Fargo, who acquired Wachovia and so the sponsorship of the Wachovia Championship, announced they would seriously cut back spending at their event.

It was clear that golf was not immune and that pay cuts would be forced upon professional golfers as sponsorships contracted. However, compensation in golf has always been more closely linked to the performance of the stock market than the economy, and the stock market globally always recovers long before the economy.

During previous slumps golf has emerged with either a new star or a new structure or tour. The US Tour as we know it today was born during the Great Depression, with the first official leading money winner having been Paul Runyon in 1934 and during the mid-1970s slump a new tour Commissioner, Deane Beman, radically restructured the tour. He arrived in his new job, as only the Tour's second Commissioner, almost exactly coincident with the great stock market trough of 1974.

In early 2009 it seemed obvious that the economic backdrop was going to continue to deteriorate for some time, however, it was also quite possible that much of that deterioration had already been factored into stock markets given their huge falls over the preceding year and a half and therefore some respite in the markets could have been expected.

Tiger's absence from the game during the period of maximum wealth destruction in the markets was obviously purely coincidental, but golf would breathe a big sigh of relief when he returned. In March 2009 the world was wondering just what "stimulus package" would finally end the miserable decline in global markets. At the same time the commentator on the Golf Channel, who described Tiger's return as "the comeback the world has been waiting for", probably had no idea just how prescient his observation was and just what a "stimulus package" Tiger's return to golf would prove to be.

TIGER'S RETURN

Tiger returned to competitive golf in early 2009 with the Dow Jones Industrial Average down forty percent from where it had been when he secured his fourteenth major in the 2008 US Open and with the golf world desperate for some good news. Expectations were high as he returned to defend his Accenture World Match Play title and an ESPN poll showed that forty-nine percent of viewers would be watching the event solely because Tiger was playing. Tiger was unsuccessful in his attempt to defend a title he had won three times before, but it was clear that he was back, and that he was healthy. The same could not be said for the markets. In the week immediately after Tiger's return the Dow continued to slide, it fell all week and eventually hit a low point on Monday March 9th, down fifty-five percent from where it had been in October 2007. It had been a horrendous seventeen months for investors, the worst decline most had ever experienced.

That day, apart from Tiger's return, there was little positive in the news, but that is the backdrop that is always seen at important low points in markets.

From that depressed level in the second week of March 2009 markets the world over rocketed higher, much to the surprise and disbelief of investors. Less than three weeks later, when Tiger teed up in the first round of the Arnold Palmer Invitational at Bay Hill in Florida, the Dow had enjoyed one of its best rallies ever, surging twenty-four percent. Admittedly this was off an historically low base, but it was the best investors had seen for a very long time. Tiger returned to form too over the next four days, and with rounds of 68, 69, 71 and 67 finished at five under par, one ahead of Sean O'Hair, Tiger retained the title despite having been out of the game for so long, it was his sixth victory in Arnold's invitational. It was his 66th tour victory, four more than Arnold Palmer himself won from 1955 to 1973 – it left him only seven behind Jack Nicklaus and sixteen behind the all time record of 82 held by Sam Snead, but Snead's winning streak spanned thirty years. The victory came in only his third event after returning from knee surgery and it was his first PGA Tour event of 2009.

To say that Tiger's return was long awaited would be a massive understatement, the Tour, his sponsors and the TV companies were all hanging out for his return. The Great Recession had devastated corporate spending on sport, art and entertainment. It was hoped that Tiger's return would prove to be the catalyst for something of a resurgence, at least in golf-related spending. Many of Tiger's sponsors, including Gatorade, Tag Hauer and Nike all launched special advertising campaigns in late February to mark his return and Cindy Davis, the President of Nike Golf summed up the reason:

Not only was Tiger's return spectacular, so too was the recovery in global investment markets.

"We knew when Tiger returned it would be a big, if not the biggest, sports story of the year. We wanted to capitalise on that."

They did, and Tiger certainly delivered with that spectacular victory and the fans were thrilled too. Surveys have shown that at times almost half the TV audience for a golf event are only there because Tiger is playing. His influence was certainly apparent at Bay Hill. NBC recorded their highest overnight golf rating since the 2008 US Open. Even more remarkable was that the audience was twenty-three percent up on the 2008 Palmer Invitational when Tiger was also victorious.

Not only was Tiger's return spectacular, so too was the recovery in global investment markets. Up to the end of February, 2009 had been a miserable year for investors with markets globally down twenty percent or more – it had been one of the worst starts to a year in history and the outlook did not look good. Nonetheless, it is important for investors to remember that markets bottom not because the news suddenly reverses from bad to good, rather markets bottom because while the news generally may continue to deteriorate it just doesn't get as bad as quickly as the majority fear.

After the victory at Bay Hill the rest of the year was almost vintage Tiger. He won five more times on the US Tour, won the season-long FedEx Cup, won the money title and was the PGA Tour Player of the Year for the tenth time. The markets also enjoyed the balance of 2009. The Dow Jones Industrial Average ended the year more than sixty percent higher than it had been at the depths of the March lows, just after Tiger had returned.

With a win in November at the J B Were Australian Masters to close his year, it seemed that 2010 was set to be another great year for Tiger and that the pursuit of his fifteenth major would continue, on the way to his ultimate target of Jack's record. The recovery in markets had also raised expectations that Great Depression II had been averted and that things were back to normal for investors. Neither quite transpired as expected but the meltdown in Tiger's personal and professional life was almost incomprehensible.

When the news of Tiger's marital infidelity transformed from tabloid gossip and rumour to fact, Tiger announced he would be withdrawing from professional golf indefinitely. So soon after his injury-induced break, and given the question marks that consequently hung over his image, this sent another shock wave through the golf and sponsorship world. The stock market also struggled through much of 2010, trading in a frustrating and broad trading range, certainly not the neat extrapolation of 2009 that so many had expected.

The year ended with a modest ten percent gain for investors but it was an even more disappointing year for Tiger and 2010 will go down in the record books as his poorest year ever as a professional. For the first time in his career he failed to win any tournaments, let alone a major.

Tiger's slump in form continued through 2011, a year that once again only delivered very modest returns to investors, less than six percent, and again Tiger was winless. What seemed his destiny just a couple of years earlier, to surpass eighteen majors, was beginning to look increasingly like a fragile dream.

Just as 2009 was Tiger's comeback year, 1975 was Jack's. As markets plunged in 1974 Jack had his worst year ever as a pro but in 1975 markets reversed dramatically to close the year up almost fifty percent from the depressed low point of late 1974. Jack had a great year too – he won five tournaments including the Masters and the US PGA, finished third in the British Open and tied seventh in the US Open. He won the money list, was Player of the Year and had the lowest stroke average he would ever achieve.

Over the next two years markets were substantially less kind to investors, rising in early 1976 before rolling over and ending 1977 at the lowest point they had been at since early 1975. Through this more difficult period for investors Jack enjoyed only modest success on the golf course winning five tour events in total but, importantly, no majors.

By the end of 1977 Jack had been a professional for sixteen seasons, in that time he had won sixty-four tour events including fourteen majors. For the first four years of his professional career Jack enjoyed the tail wind of the crescendo of a bull market, but for the next twelve years the investment environment became substantially more challenging as the market swung violently in a series of deep bear markets and strong but short recoveries.

As 2011 ended Tiger had encountered almost the identical stock market back drop. His first four years saw the culmination of a very strong bull market and then the next dozen saw the market fall and rise in an even more violent and volatile fashion than during Jack's career. Tiger had also won fourteen majors and had won seventy-one tour events.

These parallels may be nothing more than coincidence, nonetheless, they are remarkable. Whether Tiger does ultimately achieve his long-stated goal of winning more than eighteen majors only time will tell. It is worth remembering that it took Jack another nine seasons to win his final major, the 1986 Masters, and by the time he did the frustrating and volatile sideways-tracking bear market that began in 1966 had ended and a new historically rewarding bull market had begun. A bull market that would endure long enough to see Tiger through his first four years as a professional.

CHAPTER SEVEN
The Closeness of the Relationship, BUT Sometimes it's too Close

"Sudden success in golf is like the sudden acquisition of wealth. It is apt to unsettle and deteriorate the character." P.G. Wodehouse

Golf and business are closely related, and have been since both "great games" came into being, but this relationship hasn't always been healthy. Golf has always had a special relationship with corporate executives, and this has undoubtedly been one of the reasons why stock market returns and the rewards to top professionals have been so close for so long. This relationship has also resulted in executive compensation mirroring almost perfectly the ebb and flow of the incomes of leading professional golfers. This is entirely understandable, and there should be nothing wrong with this closely intertwined relationship. But sadly history is littered with scandals and scams that have been perpetrated or initiated on or around the golf course and there are numerous examples of executives that exploited their positions to benefit their golf, or allowed their golf to distract them from their business. Finally, it is now clear that golf played a central part in the biggest fraud of all time – the $65 billion Bernie Madoff Ponzi scheme. The relationship between the two "great games" is indeed close, but sometimes it has become far too close.

THE RICH GET RICHER!

At the end of each calendar year the financial media, and in some cases the general media, enter into the fortune-telling business, or at least the collation of other's forecasts. They survey leading financial and investment commentators and ask "What is going to happen over the next twelve months?" This can be entertaining but should not be relied upon as anything like a blueprint of the future, far from it as invariably the forecasts hover around being an extrapolation of what has recently been happening. If the prior year has ended well it is usual that this more constructive pattern is forecast to continue, equally if the year has ended badly it is likely that the "experts" would be looking for some continuation of this "challenging" period before more "normal" rising markets return. Ahead of what would become known as the Global Financial Crisis the focus of the year-end commentary had a slightly different tone.

After a healthy year for most investment markets in 2006, still almost a year ahead of the peak that would ultimately mark the beginning of the GFC, rather than forecasting still rosier times ahead, as would have been normal, the financial media reflected a strong sense of resentment, a most unusual characteristic in financial journalism. It was focused upon just how much richer the rich were getting on the back of the dominant investment trends throughout 2006.

This shift in focus was highlighted by a number of totally unrelated events ranging from a severance package of $214 million for one American CEO through to the bonuses that were paid at the global investment bank, Goldman Sachs. Goldman Sachs' year-end bonus pool totalled $16.5 billion, or an average of more than $600,000 per salaried employee. Naturally this pool was not "shared" quite equally: the CEO received more than $50 million. These outlandish bonuses caused the cleaners in the firm's London office, who were on a basic six pounds and twenty pence an hour contract, to threaten to strike.

This new tone of resentment over the gap between the rich and everyone else was clearly troubling, and in some ways was reminiscent of the focus on corporate corruption in the wake of Enron's collapse a few years earlier. But what does it have to do with golf?

As 2006 ended the sports media were also focusing on year-end reviews and forecasts for the New Year and, like in the financial media, money and wealth was a subject of great interest. In golf, in addition to the rankings on all the various tours by money won, Golf Digest compiles its top 50 global earners that takes into account both on and off course earnings and not surprisingly Tiger Woods came out comfortably on top. That year Tiger Woods and Nike had announced another five-year deal. Tiger's first deal with Nike was worth $8 million a year for five years, his second in 2001 rose to a reported $20 million a year and his extension for 2006 was expected to soar even further. The sums involved for top golf professionals, and Tiger in particular, had by 2006 become staggering. In each of the prior four years, Tiger had enjoyed a total income in excess of $80 million and he was well on the way to fulfilling one of his late father's earliest predictions – that Tiger would be the world's first sporting billionaire.

Thirty years ago on course earnings for professional golfers were an essential part of their total income, and endorsement contracts came predominantly from golf equipment manufacturers and golf-related companies. Now, at least for the top professionals, prize money can be as little as one-tenth of their total income, and the type of companies attracted to golf and golf endorsements has exploded way beyond the golf industry. Entertainment companies, car manufacturers, watch makers and finance and investment companies all now sponsor individual players as well as tournaments.

The result has been that at the same time as prize money has soared, total compensation for top golf professionals has risen even faster. Therein lies an intriguing parallel with the corporate world.

Much of the resentment commented upon earlier is as a result of the ever-growing gap between the average worker and those at the top. Kevin Murphy of the University of Southern California has tracked this gap. Kevin has taken the pay of the average worker and divided it into the pay of the average American CEO going back as far as 1970.

In 1970, the average American CEO earned about 30 times what the average worker received, a healthy and potentially justifiable multiple. However, since then the multiple has risen dramatically, to the point that at the end of 2005 the average CEO was earning in excess of 100 times what the average worker was earning. In 1970, the average CEO's compensation totalled about $180,000, and stock options were virtually unheard of. This rose to more than $3 million by 2005 when it stood at 100 times the average worker's compensation. If CEO stock options are included, this figure jumped to closer to 500 times the average worker. With these enormous multiples in mind, it is worth remembering that the legendary financier J. P. Morgan once said that he would never lend money to a company whose highest paid employee made more than twenty times the lowest as, in his view, it was unstable.

Over the same period, the top US (professional male) golfer saw his cash winnings rise from $157,000 in 1970 (when Lee Trevino topped the money list) to Tigers $10 million in 2005. The growth in both CEO compensation and leading golf money winner's totals tracked each other extremely closely from 1970 through to 2005.

Since 2005, when Murphy published his research, the close relationship has continued. Steven Kaplan at the Booth School of Business at the University of Chicago published an analysis of the average compensation of S&P500 Chief Executive Officers from 1993 through to 2009. Both the average and median CEO's compensation rocketed about four times from 1993 through to the very early 2000s. Since then their total compensation on average has declined, very much in synch with the stock market. Top golfers earnings fell in the wake of the bursting of the Dot Com bubble in the early 2000s, so too did the earnings of CEOs before they again rose to almost match their previous peak by 2006 or 2007, just as golfers incomes did. From there both the leading golfer and the average S&P500 CEO's incomes have fallen dramatically. The average CEO's income has slipped from just over $16 million to about $8 million and the leading golfer's winnings have declined from $10 million to less than $7 million.

The still growing sense of resentment about the corporate world is not apparent among professional golfers. If anything, the opposite may be true as players like Phil Mickelson have publicly acknowledged the gratitude they feel towards Tiger for increasing the overall pie. It may also be the case that the charitable fundraising that golf generally, and professional golf in particular, is responsible for distracting some of the attention that might otherwise have been focused on the outrageous expansion in prize money available. In the US golfing events, including the PGA Tour, raise more money for charity than all other sports combined. *Golf Digest* estimates that the PGA Tour raises about $120 million annually but that this is only a tiny fraction of the more than $3.5 billion raised in grass-root charity golf events throughout America each year.

The real question is how sustainable the current growth rate in both professional golf compensation and corporate CEO compensation can be. Both can continue to grow, but as long as they continue to grow faster than the overall pool of compensation available, or the overall economy, that growth has to come at the expense of something or someone else. Ultimately, taking a larger and larger piece of an, albeit growing, pie, year after a year, is not sustainable. It is also the case that the sustainability of such enormous levels of compensation is brought into question if, as the P G Wodehouse quote at the beginning of this chapter points out, ones character becomes unsettled or deteriorates.

When one reads that quote it is hard not to think of Tiger Woods. He undoubtedly enjoyed a sudden acquisition of almost unimaginable wealth – in 2009, immediately prior to his personal life imploding, his total compensation was $121,915,196. After the "deterioration in his character" became public his total compensation fell to $74 million in 2010 and in 2011 his total earnings were "only" $64 million. More than virtually any Hollywood celebrity and probably only beaten by a handful of CEOs and hedge fund managers but still down almost fifty percent from his peak just two years earlier.

PERKS OF THE JOB

Many Chief Executives are also passionate golfers, in fact for many CEOs it is difficult to tell when their business day is over and their personal life begins, so much of what they do is in some way or another related to their business, either closely or indirectly. It is certainly the case that a huge number of deals have taken place on the golf course throughout history, and that golf can be a very useful tool in the business world. However, the question that has to be asked is when does a personal passion justifiably become a business commitment and expense?

Almost a quarter of a century ago, in 1988, the world's then largest corporate takeover was about to take place. It was the leveraged buyout of the consumer giant RJR Nabisco. The intrigue and manoeuvrings that accompanied this deal have been fabulously documented in the long-time bestseller *Barbarians at the Gate,* a book that gives a fascinating insight into both the deal that was put together by Kohlberg, Kravis and Roberts and the target company, RJR Nabisco. From the earliest pages it is clear that Ross Johnson, the CEO, had a love with, and fascination of, celebrity in general and golf stars in particular. The company's payroll included such golfing luminaries as Ben Crenshaw, Fuzzy Zoeller and Jack Nicklaus. These players in return for occasional games with key customers and other public relations activities received between $300,000 a year in Zoeller's case, through to one million dollars for the Golden Bear. This was at a time when the world's leading money winner had yet to win one million dollars in a single season, (in 1987 Curtis Strange won a then record $925,941 almost fifty percent more than any player had ever won in a single season) and made Jack Nicklaus the second highest paid employee in the entire company.

The book goes further in outlining the possible blurring of the boundary between the company's interests and those of its CEO with a detailed description of what became known as the RJR Air Force, a suite of executive jets that ferried executives and sports stars across the United States seemingly on a whim. The relaxed, even cavalier, attitude of CEO Johnson to the expenses associated with this behaviour is captured in what apparently became his catch phrase, *"A few million dollars are lost in the sands of time!"*

That some cost cutting would be possible in a restructured company when the takeover was complete is an understatement. Nonetheless the RJR Nabisco story illustrates just how closely intertwined the interests of golfers and the corporate world can become. So was this just a one off example of corporate negligence in the frenzied excitement of the 1980s or could similar behaviour still occur?

It is unlikely that anything on the scale of RJR Nabisco would happen now, however, it seems that senior executive interest in golf may still be causing some blurring of the boundaries between personal and business interests.

In 2005 the *Wall Street Journal* published a marvellous example of investigative journalism that relied heavily on the access reporters had through the US Golf Association's handicapping website to the dates and locations of various corporate executives' golfing activities. The article was titled:

THE CEO'S PRIVATE GOLF SHUTTLE

The article mentioned, and was almost certainly inspired by, some research published in March 2005 by then Associate Professor at New York's Stern School of Business, David Yermack. His paper was titled:

FLIGHTS OF FANCY:
Corporate Jets, CEO Perquisites, and Inferior Shareholder Returns

The primary aim of the paper was to explore the relationship between the amount of use a corporate CEO makes of the company's private jets for personal use and the performance of the company's share price, and he concluded:

The central result of this study is that CEOs' disclosed personal use of company aircraft is associated with severe and significant under-performance of their employers' stocks. Firms that disclose personal aircraft use by the CEO under-perform market benchmarks by about 4 percent or 400 basis points per year.

This is obviously a substantial underperformance, particularly given that he also pointed out that throughout the boom of the 1990s personal use of corporate aircraft by CEOs grew explosively, more than tripling from 1993 through to 2002, the sample period of his study.

What was most interesting in Yermack's paper was the close relationship he found between personal use of the company plane and the CEO's interest in golf. He wrote:

Firms disclosing the aircraft perk tend to be larger, pay their CEOs more, and have CEOs with lower ownership who are less likely to belong to the company's founding family. Also, these CEOs are about twice as likely to belong to "long distance" golf clubs that would require air travel to reach.

He established this connection by reviewing the handicap and membership details maintained by the United States Golf Association:

The U.S. Golf Association maintains an Internet database of the playing records of millions of golfers who choose to register with the association in order to establish a sanctioned handicap. The database also identifies golf clubs or country clubs where each individual is a member. In my sample, 42.8 percent of the CEOs appear in the USGA database, and a significant number — 17.2 percent of the overall sample — have country club memberships in locales very far from headquarters, mainly in the states of Florida, California, Colorado, or Massachusetts.

He concluded that if a CEO belonged to a golf club that was located a long-distance from the company headquarters then their personal use of the company aircraft increased markedly.

Whether there is anything wrong with a CEO using the company jet to facilitate regular long-distance golf games is for others to decide, but clearly the market takes a dim view of it given the marked underperformance mentioned above. In a post-GFC world some of this behaviour may have waned, but if it has it is likely only a temporary decline. It is also interesting to note one of Yermack's final comments:

Finally, company planes have played a central role in some of the most notorious corporate disclosures involving managerial excess, whether prompted by disciplinary hostile takeovers (such as RJR-Nabisco2) or prosecutions for fraud.

Just as any golfer's scores, dates, times and courses played are available to the general public on the USGA website so too are many of the flight times and dates and passengers and destinations of many corporate jets. What the investigative journalists at the Wall Street Journal did was marry up the records of both corporate jet flights and rounds of golf of a number of high profile Chief Executive Officers. The overlapping nature of the two was indeed revealing. It's not necessarily the case that these executives were doing anything wrong, all the flights were logged and recorded as they should have been, and in most cases the executive was liable to pay some tax for the benefit received, however, this cost is minimal compared to the cost of running an executive jet and in many cases less than an economy air fare would have been.

It is undoubtedly true that many senior executives are on call virtually twenty-four hours a day, and the corporate jet may in many cases be a mobile office, but all these executives are handsomely rewarded for the roles they fulfil. That many senior executives have a real passion, and in some case a real ability, for golf is obvious. As mentioned earlier this goes some way to explaining the close relationship that has always existed between the fortunes of golf, the fortunes of business and the fortunes of investment markets.

However, the "perk" of a Private Golf Shuttle may be stretching the relationship between business and private life a little too far and blurring the ultimately necessary distinction between the two.

In addition to profiling the personal use of company jets by a number of well-known executives the article also quoted Charles Elson, director of the Weinberg Center for Corporate Governance at the University of Delaware who called it "disgusting" that a company might guarantee its CEO one hundred hours of free personal flight time, and went on to say, "A corporate aircraft isn't supposed to be a shuttle to a vacation home. We pay CEOs enough. They can afford to pay to fly to their vacation homes".

A sentiment that would no doubt be shared by many in a post-GFC world, and as the GFC was approaching the USGA's records would once again embarrass a number of high profile CEOs.

WALL STREET, GOLF AND THE GLOBAL FINANCIAL CRISIS

Following on from, and maybe even inspired by, the investigative work of the *Wall Street Journal* many journalists began to study and write about the golfing exploits of the immensely paid CEOs of Wall Street through the build-up to what we would all eventually come to know as the Global Financial Crisis.

Through much of the second half of 2007 the world's financial markets displayed turmoil and volatility the like of which had not been seen for several years. This marked an abrupt end to what had been one of the most stable and rewarding periods for investors ever. Up until then markets for just about everything, including commodities, shares, art and real estate had been soaring. Whether the abrupt change in the performance of so many investment markets indicated more challenging times ahead only time would tell, what that period of turmoil did do however, was to once again bring into the spotlight the close relationship between golf and investment markets.

The unwinding of so many markets came about as a result of investors being rudely reminded that risk has a price and that there is no such thing as a free lunch. This, on top of the explosion of increasingly complex derivative products that were created by highly paid financial engineers, meant that some kind of financial accident was almost inevitable. And financial accidents there certainly were, but what possible connection could there be between the financial turmoil and golf?

The first link to golf came from the investment firm of Bear Stearns. It was in June 2007, when a couple of Bear Stearns hedge funds began to plunge, that the extent and enormity of the fallout from the collapse in the US sub-prime lending market began to become apparent.

Throughout June the extent to which Bear Stearns was affected became increasingly obvious with each day that passed and the stock market took a lot of notice. Having traded at more than $170 earlier in the year the shares of Bear Stearns plunged with the fall being particularly dramatic through July and August when they fell below $100.

With his company's share price collapsing, and in the midst of the biggest hedge fund rescue in almost a decade, the company's CEO, James Cayne, never took his eye off the ball, but possibly it wasn't the right ball at the right time.

At the time Cayne was a very keen golfer and possibly the wealthiest Wall Street executive with a reported net worth in excess of a billion dollars. As sections of his company were falling apart around him he never missed one of his regular Thursday and Friday rounds of golf. The New York Times published a chronicle of Mr Cayne's golf alongside the action of his company's shares. His golf seemed totally unaffected by what was going on in the office, even though his spokesman explained that he was constantly in touch, even on the golf course.

On November 1, 2007, with what would become known as the GFC beginning to really take hold, the *Wall Street Journal* ran an article under the headline:

BEAR CEO'S HANDLING OF CRISIS RAISES ISSUES
Cayne on Golf Links, 10-Day Bridge Trip Amid Summer Turmoil

The article began:

A crisis at Bear Stearns Cos. this summer came to a head in July. Two Bear hedge funds were hemorrhaging value. Investors were clamoring to get their money back. Lenders to the funds were demanding more collateral. Eventually, both funds collapsed.

During 10 critical days of this crisis -- one of the worst in the securities firm's 84-year history -- Bear's chief executive wasn't near his Wall Street office. James Cayne was playing in a bridge tournament in Nashville, Tenn., without a cellphone or an email device. In one closely watched competition, his team placed in the top third.

As Bear's fund meltdown was helping spark this year's mortgage-market and credit convulsions, Mr. Cayne at times missed key events. At a tense August conference call with investors, he left after a few opening words and listeners didn't know when he returned. In summer weeks, he typically left the office on Thursday afternoon and spent Friday at his New Jersey golf club, out of touch for stretches, according to associates and golf records. In the critical month of July, he spent 10 of the 21 workdays out of the office, either at the bridge event or golfing, according to golf, bridge and hotel records.

As the pressure intensified on the firm to raise money for the struggling funds Mr Cayne began his summer ritual as the *Wall Street Journal* reported:

About this time, Mr. Cayne began his summertime ritual of taking a helicopter from New York City to Deal, N.J., on Thursdays to make a late-afternoon golf game at the exclusive Hollywood Golf Club, associates say. (He pays for the 17-minute, $1,700 trips himself, one person says.) After spending the night in his vacation home nearby, associates add, Mr. Cayne generally hits the golf course again Friday morning for another 18 holes, followed by 8 a.m. tee-offs on Saturday and Sunday. Friends say that after his Saturday game, he often heads back to his local home for several hours of online poker and bridge and to play with his grandchildren.

By early June creditors began to seize assets that backed loans for the funds but:

Mr. Cayne was on the golf course in New Jersey part of that day, a Friday, having left the office Thursday afternoon, according to a Web site that tracks individuals' golf scores.

In late July the troubled funds were forced into bankruptcy, but that was not going to mark the end of Bear's problems, in fact they were just beginning as another fund was facing similar demands from investors for their money back.

At the same time investors in Bear Stearns itself were beginning to get concerned, but after a week that saw the Bear disaster cause the market to plunge and senior Bear executives to resign Mr Cayne showed no such anxiety:

The following day, a Saturday, Mr. Cayne scored a respectable 88 at the Hollywood golf course, according to the golf Web site. But for Bear, things seemed to be falling apart that weekend. Major clients of the firm's prime brokerage division were threatening to pull their business.

Bear Stearns' share price plunged and so too did Mr Cayne's wealth. It is reported that when he finally sold his holding in the company to J P Morgan in March of 2008, just days ahead of their taking over the entire company, he received just $61 million. Still a tidy sum but a world apart from the almost one billion dollars that his holding had once been worth. In the aftermath of the GFC, and the demise of Bear Stearns, it seems that Mr Cayne no longer benefited from the solace and peace that the golf course offered, at least according to the Golf Handicap and Information Network (GHIN) – he seems now to rarely break 100.

Soon after the events at Bear Stearns an even higher profile Wall Street CEO was caught on the golf course when all hell was breaking loose back in the office. If Bear Stearns was the first Wall Street giant to have been walloped by the turmoil then Merrill Lynch was, at least up to that point, the most damaged. Its shares had fallen even further than Bear Stearns and the company recorded the largest hit against earnings for losses related to the then still early stages of the GFC. For their third quarter Merrill Lynch took a staggering $8.4 billion dollar charge, more than twice the amount that any other firm had so far taken and equivalent to more than thirteen percent of the company's entire share market value. This announcement caused the shares of Merrill to fall but the question that shareholders, and it seems many journalists too, were asking was – where was the CEO, Stan O'Neal, while all this was happening?

The unfortunate answer, at least for Mr. O'Neal, was, on the golf course! Of course he wasn't there the entire time but it seems he managed to get in more rounds than most fully employed workers would be able to.

From August 12 through to the end of September 2007, as the third quarter was coming to an end and his company was haemorrhaging money, Mr O'Neal managed to log twenty rounds of golf, and it seems that, like for Mr Cayne, the golf was a welcome distraction from the problems at work. Through the troubled third quarter for Merrill Lynch Mr O'Neal's handicap fell from 10.2 to 9.1.

In the end the write-offs and the collapsing share price were too much for the Merrill Lynch board to take and Mr O'Neal was forced to resign. This no doubt freed up even more time for him to work on his game, and his only distraction was what to do with his $161 million dollar retirement package!

STANLEY ONEAL

METROPOLITAN GOLF ASSOCIATION
PURCHASE GOLF CLUB OF

USGA HANDICAP INDEX HISTORY

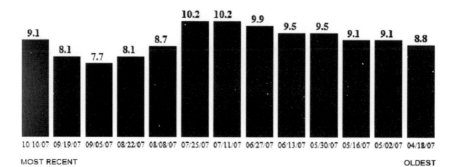

					10.2	10.2	9.9						
9.1				8.7				9.5	9.5	9.1	9.1	8.8	
	8.1	7.7	8.1										

10/10/07 09/19/07 09/05/07 08/22/07 08/08/07 07/25/07 07/11/07 06/27/07 06/13/07 05/30/07 05/16/07 05/02/07 04/18/07

MOST RECENT   OLDEST

Metropolitan Golf Association
Purchase Golf Club of
Name : Stanley Oneal

9.1
Effective 10/10/2007

CLICK HERE FOR
MOST RECENT
SCORES

 View Index History

 Course Handicap Calculator

Score History

Used	T	Date	Score	CR/Slope	Diff.	Course Name
	H	9/30/07	88	72.0/140	12.9	Purchase Country Club
	H	9/29/07	89	72.0/140	13.7	Purchase Country Club
*	AI	9/22/07	80	70.7/123	8.5	Waccabuc Country Club
	AI	9/22/07	89	71.1/133	15.2	Shinnecock Hills Golf Club
	AI	9/22/07	90	72.0/140	14.5	Purchase Country Club
	AI	9/15/07	90	72.4/140	14.2	
*	H	9/3/07	84	72.0/140	9.7	Purchase Country Club
	H	9/2/07	91	72.0/140	15.3	Purchase Country Club
	H	9/1/07	87	71.6/133	13.1	Vineyard Golf Club
*	H	8/31/07	83	71.6/133	9.7	Vineyard Golf Club
*	H	8/29/07	85	71.6/133	11.4	Vineyard Golf Club
*	H	8/26/07	85	71.6/133	11.4	Vineyard Golf Club
*	AI	8/26/07	83	70.5/133	10.6	
	AI	8/19/07	86	71.9/133	12.0	
	AI	8/19/07	85	71.5/134	11.4	
	AI	8/19/07	93	72.1/132	17.9	
*	AI	8/19/07	80	70.5/133	8.1	
*	AI	8/18/07	83	71.1/133	10.1	
*	H	8/12/07	86	72.0/140	11.3	Purchase Country Club
*	A	8/12/07	76	70.8/137	4.3	Away Score Posted at Home Club

Score Type: H - Home, A - Away, T - Tournament,
P - Penalty, C - Combined 9H, I - Internet

Stan O'Neal may have resigned but sadly Merrill Lynch went the same way as Bear Stearns and was eventually acquired, for a tiny fraction of its once lofty valuation, by Bank America.

At the height of the Global Financial Crisis, and at the same time as journalists were investigating which CEOs were playing how much golf, the Bespoke Investment Group posted the recent scores and handicaps of five Wall Street CEOs in the hope of discovering whether there was a correlation or relationship between golfing ability and business success. The results were as follows:

CEOs Ranked by Handicap
    1. Stanley O'Neal (9.9) Merrill Lynch
    2. Richard Fuld (10.3) Lehman Brothers
    3. James Cayne (15.9) Bear Stearns
    4. John Mack (17.0) Morgan Stanley
    5. Lloyd Blankfein (32.1) Goldman Sachs

CEOs Ranked by Percent Change in Stock Price This Golf Season
    1. Lloyd Blankfein (+6.9%)
    2. Richard Fuld (+3.14%)
    3. Stanley O'Neal (-1.3%)
    4. James Cayne (-3.49%)
    5. John Mack (-9.86%)

There doesn't appear to be any relationship except that Lloyd Blankfein had the best-performing share price over that golf season and was easily the worst golfer. It is also interesting to note that Blankfein is the only one still employed in the same role at the same company. Most disconcerting, at least from a golfing perspective, is that the three best golfers – Stan O'Neal, Richard Fuld and James Cayne all made it onto Conde Nast *Portfolio Magazine*'s list of the twenty worst CEOs of all time. To be fair the article was written right at the depths of the GFC, in early 2009, so the damage that all three had overseen was still making the headlines. However, the list also included Jay Gould from the late 1800s about whom the magazine wrote: "When it comes to unscrupulous behaviour, Gould makes Milken (Mike Milken the disgraced former junk bond 'King' of Drexel Burnham) look like a sweetheart".

O'Neal was "only" eighteenth on this hall of shame but Cayne was fourth and Fuld had the unenviable privilege of coming first. Around the same time as Wall Street CEOs were playing golf while all around them, their organisations were collapsing, another thread in golf's close, and often too close, relationship with Wall Street was about to be revealed.

PONZI AND GOLF

Towards the end of 2008, in the second week of December, news that shocked the world was breaking in New York. It first broke on the financial pages but quickly spread to the mainstream news. It concerned what will probably go down in history as the biggest Ponzi scheme (or fraud) ever involving fifty to sixty-five billion dollars.

Since the 1920s, at a time when golf was undoubtedly a game of honour and Bobby Jones was alarmed to be praised for calling a penalty upon himself, any business fraud or scam based upon early "investors" being paid-out by a necessarily growing number of later investors has been known as a Ponzi scheme. Such pyramid schemes are named after Charles Ponzi, who in 1920 launched a scheme offering returns of fifty percent in 45 days or one hundred percent in 90 days. From a very modest start, the scheme grew at an alarming rate with Ponzi hiring "agents" who received commissions on all new money they attracted. After a few months people were mortgaging their homes to invest in the scheme as word spread that early investors had been paid out. All pyramid schemes eventually fall apart and Ponzi's did too upon his arrest in August of 1920. At the time, seventeen thousand people had "invested" tens of millions of dollars. Many were ruined.

Given the importance of integrity and honour in golf one might wonder what possible connection there could be between Charles Ponzi and golf. Unfortunately, this question was all too clearly answered by the scheme that blew open that December.

On December 10, 2008 seventy-year-old Bernard Madoff, one of the most respected men on Wall Street and a former non-executive chairman of NASDAQ, confessed to his two sons that he had been operating a $50 billion Ponzi scheme through his Bernard L Madoff Securities business. He told his sons that he was finished, that he had nothing and that it had all been just one big lie. For years Madoff had appeared to be a successful investor. He never offered his clients returns that were too-good-to-be-true, such as Ponzi boasted, rather, what he offered was good, but not spectacular, returns of around twelve percent per year. Most incredible of all was that he never appeared to lose money. It didn't seem to matter whether markets went up or down Madoff still made his usual return. To very wealthy investors, such healthy and stable returns were highly sought after. However, Madoff was not open to take just anyone's money. To have your money looked after by Madoff became something of a badge of honour amongst the rich and famous.

Bernie Madoff enjoyed his golf, and it was apparently not uncommon for new investors to be invited to invest with Madoff while he was at one of his golfing haunts on Long Island or in Florida. In fact, it is rumoured that some wealthy individuals joined certain golf clubs just in the hope of meeting Bernie and having the opportunity to invest with him. The list of Madoff's victims reads like a who's who of the rich and famous.

The golf connection between Madoff and his clients and prospective clients was neatly captured in a Golf.com story that ran in May of 2009 under the headline:

Bernie Madoff's golf memberships provided the perfect venue to run the largest Ponzi scheme in history

The article focused upon one individual who had been caught in Madoff's scam and went on to summarise the breadth and depth of his activities and the fallout from them on golfers and golf clubs:

"They say to trust your swing," she says. "But it's hard to know what else you can trust these days.

As the summer golf season kicks into gear, a similar lament echoes across many of the country's poshest clubs, where fallout from history's largest Ponzi scheme has struck particularly close to home. Of the thousands of investors swindled by financier Bernie Madoff, scores were golfers, as was the scam's architect himself. Through his own memberships, and those of associates who wrangled investors for him, Madoff enjoyed access to swank private clubs in Florida, New York, Boston and beyond. He used their grounds to prey on the game's fat cats, whose trust (and trusts) was the lifeblood of his ploy. Some of Madoff's alleged victims were household names, including four-time major winner Raymond Floyd, whose name appears on a list of Madoff clients that was released as part of a court filing. But most were merely wealthy, pursuing their pastime in privileged anonymity on the same fairways where Madoff chased his ball.

For many of these clubs, already staggered by a deepening recession, the scandal hit like a body blow. Up and down the East Coast, club members have resigned in droves, some casualties of the economy but many of them cleaned out by a man who'd changed his spikes beside them in their locker rooms.

Last December, days after Madoff confessed, management at Glen Oaks Country Club on Long Island (where Madoff's brother, Peter, was a member and Madoff himself played) called an emergency meeting at which some 20 members resigned on the spot, according to a veteran club pro with knowledge of Glen Oaks. (The club did not return several phone calls seeking comment.)

At North Shore Country Club, another Long Island haunt full of Madoff investors, membership has reportedly plummeted from 175 to 110 in the wake of the scandal, driving speculation that the 95-year-old club might not live to see its 100th birthday. And at Palm Beach Country Club in Florida, the club hardest hit by the scheme, staff responded to news of the scandal by stripping Madoff's name from his locker and shipping his sticks to his New York penthouse – small consolation to members who reportedly could no longer afford their dues.

"It's hard to overestimate the impact that this has had on the golf world," says Casey Alexander, a senior golf-industry analyst at Gilford

Securities in New York. "If you talked to members of almost any high-end club, you'd find someone who was affected, or who knows someone who was."

Two months earlier, in May of 2009, the *Wall Street Journal* had also highlighted the impact of the Madoff scam on golf clubs. The headline ran;

Latest Madoff Victim: Gold Coast Country Club

The *Wall Street Journal* focused upon the plight of the Woodcrest Club on Long Island's smart North Shore, in the wake of the scam and the loss of members, apparently "bamboozled" by Madoff, the club faced $700,000 in bills to vendors that it could not pay. It had no option but to file for bankruptcy.

The real tragedy of the whole Madoff affair was not that many wealthy individuals became less wealthy, or that golf and golf clubs played such a central role, but that much of the money he supposedly "looked after" was for charities and the majority of that money has not been, and will almost certainly never be, recouped no matter how long a jail sentence Madoff serves.

With the benefit of hindsight it is possible to speculate that some questions as to Madoff's previously impeccable and highly respected character should have been asked and the clues lay in his golf and the scores he reported. It wasn't only the "returns" that Madoff reported to existing clients that were perpetually steady!

CNBC, the business TV network, uncovered a section of Madoff's golfing history that involved twenty rounds played at three of his clubs: the Atlantic Club and Fresh Meadow Country Club on Long Island and the Palm Beach Country Club in Florida. Virtually every round was right on his handicap 12, very few golfers, let alone 12 handicappers play exactly to their handicap every time – but twelve it seems was the magic number for Madoff, it was exactly the return, twelve percent, that he guaranteed to new investors and apparently delivered to existing ones. As the noted American novelist Paul Gallico once wrote in the *New York Times* "If there is larceny in a man, golf will bring it out."

It is clear there was in Madoff and it seems golf did!

That Madoff's Ponzi scheme came unstuck when it did is not that surprising, what was of great surprise was the sheer scale of his scheme. Corruption and fraud always tend to flourish during boom times as usually fewer and fewer questions get asked if seemingly everyone is doing better and better. If no one is being hurt then no damage is being done so why look for a problem! Unfortunately it is when the music stops that the problems begin. Once markets start to fall the more a reason for the fall is sought, and once markets really fall the greater the need for someone or something to blame.

Prior to Madoff and the GFC this reason-seeking behaviour was seen as stock markets plunged in the early 2000s, after the technology bubble burst. As markets were falling in their worst decline since the 1970s the frauds and scams at Worldcom and Enron came to light and eventually lengthy prison terms were handed out to those seen as being the perpetrators of the frauds. It is important to realise that those earlier scams did not cause the markets to collapse and neither did Madoff bring about the GFC. In all cases the fraudulent behaviour had been taking place for years, and had likely been fuelled by the preceding boom, but when the "music" of ever-rising markets stopped the cracks appeared and the questions began to be asked.

It is said that there is never only one cockroach and whenever a boom turns to a bust, as they all eventually do, there never seems to be only one fraudster or scammer exploiting the boom and investors' greed. In the wake of the Madoff revelations, there have been a slew of, admittedly smaller, scams and Ponzi schemes that have come to light and it is not surprising that golf has regularly been involved.

In the immediate wake of the Madoff revelations, in early 2009, the *LA Times* reported:

Six O.C. men charged in $52-million investment scam
The operators of Carolina Development conned more than 1,000 in a Ponzi scheme, California Atty. Gen. Jerry Brown's office says.

Six Orange County men face criminal fraud charges in an alleged $52-million *investment scam that was said to promise big profits from luxury developments next to golf courses designed by Arnold Palmer, Jack Nicklaus and Greg Norman.*

Still the behaviour continues and still golf is often involved. In the second half of 2011 James Davis Risher pleaded guilty to running a $22 million Ponzi scheme in Florida. The scheme began in 2007 with many of the "investors" being seduced into his "The Preservation of Principal Fund" whilst competing in especially organised golf tournaments.

The relationship between golf and investment markets can become too close but this problem is not confined to America, or to the west — it seems it is a global phenomenon.

CHINA, GOLF AND CORRUPTION

Golf, surprisingly, may have a very long history in China. While it is generally agreed that what we now know as golf first emerged in Scotland 600 years ago there are a variety of claims that a forerunner of golf existed substantially earlier. These claims include those that "chuiwan" was the basis from which golf evolved. "Chui" means striking and "wan" means small ball and chuiwan was apparently played between the 8th and 14th centuries. A Ming Dynasty scroll dating from 1368 appears to show a member of the Chinese Imperial court aiming to sink a small ball in a hole by hitting it with a club.

Whether or not golf did once have deep origins in China is a somewhat irrelevant question when one thinks of the modern game as for the majority of the last one hundred years, during which golf has flourished, It was a sport that was virtually unknown in China as it was banned by the communist party on account of it being too bourgeois.

The first course in mainland China, the Chung Shan Hot Spring Golf Club based on a design by Arnold Palmer, was not started until 1984 and was followed by what can only be described as an explosion in golf course construction. From that first course in 1984 there are now more than 600 courses in China and the industry is growing at an annual rate of twenty-five to thirty percent. Currently there are around 300,000 golfers in China – however, this is expected to grow to more than 20 million by the year 2020.

What is most intriguing about these growth figures is that technically it is still illegal to build a golf course in China. Then Premier Wen Jiabo stated at the 2007 National People's Congress that the construction of new golf courses was not only a waste of public money but also an illegal use of space. As a result he announced that contracts to build new courses should be highly discouraged. Currently the government imposes a twenty-four percent tax on golf clubs. Despite this "hurdle" it is clear that golf continues to flourish in China, it seems that the relationship between big business and golf is just as close, if not even closer, in China as it is in so much of the rest of the world. As a result the "relationship" can sometimes prove too close. This "closeness" was explored in an article in May 2011 in the *Financial Times:*

Golf course boom points to China corruption

The article described the notable proliferation of golf courses since the supposed "official" ban on their construction was put in place. At that time China had about 170 golf courses but since the ban was put in place in 2004 that number has more than tripled to 600. The ban was introduced to preserve farmland and water and to prevent peasants being thrown off their land to make way for the developments.

According to the article the existence of many of these new courses is evidence of both the weakness of central government but more importantly to the ability of those who are rich, powerful and well connected to get around the law. One course cited in the article, Qinghe Bay, is owned by one of the country's largest steel producers and when the journalist asked one of the marketing executives at the club how the club was able to come into being they were told that they didn't know how to answer and that it wasn't convenient to take the enquiry any further.

Upon further investigation it seemed that local government officials were almost always involved in the development of illegal golf courses. It seems that so long as developers are well-connected then illegal courses will continue to be built in China.

That the relationship between golf and business may at times get too close in China, just as it seems to everywhere else, raises the question as to whether any of the other parallels between the two "great games" can be found in China.

Unfortunately it is still too early in golf's development in China to explore the relationship between the local stock market and the money in professional golf, however, it is interesting to note what has happened since 2005. In late 2005 the Chinese stock market, as measured by the Shanghai Composite Index, began a meteoric rise of historical proportions. After drifting down from more than 2000 to around 1000 over the prior three years, the market suddenly exploded and over the next two years rose six fold in value! The index soared in a virtual straight line from just 1000 to 6000, peaking in late 2007. This incredible rise understandably attracted global media attention and suddenly China became the hottest market for international investors, *Wealth Daily* ran the following story in late 2007:

China Stock Market Boom
CHINA BOOM CONTINUES WITH NEW STOCKS AND CONSUMERS
By Sam Hopkins, Tuesday, October 16th, 2007

China now has the fourth-largest market cap in the world. The Shanghai, Shenzhen, and Hong Kong exchanges are all beating the pants off of Wall Street. But this week's Communist Party Congress tells me there's plenty of room to grow.

Who would have thought twenty years ago that we would be looking to any Marxist body for bullish indicators on the world's most impressive economy? Well, it's a new century and China's economy is bursting forth at 11% growth per year. If you're not in on it, you're leaving heaps of money on the table. But it's not too late to follow this waking dragon to prosperity.

President Hu Jintao announced three major goals at the five-yearly congress:
- *Quadruple China's per capita GDP by 2020 from 2000 levels.*
- *Reduce resource consumption and ramp up environmental protection.*
- *List the stocks of up to 50 state-owned enterprises for public trading.*

With such cheerleading it is not surprising that the market was attracting so much attention and through this remarkable boom professional golf in China went along for the ride.

At the start of the boom China hosted its first HSBC Champions tournament at the Sheshan Golf Club in Shanghai, four years later this would become a World Golf Championship event. Nonetheless that first tournament in 2005 was certainly big and attracted substantial media coverage as David Howell of England edged out the then world number one, Tiger Woods, for the title. As the market continued to rocket higher more tournaments came to China. In 2007 the Asian Tour added the Beijing Open and the Media China Classic and the LPGA Tour announced that they were going to hold the inaugural Grand China Air event. Finally in 2007 China was awarded the hosting of the World Cup of Golf at Mission Hills and the event is now known as the Omega Mission Hills World Cup. But then the bubble that was the Chinese market burst and as share prices plunged through 2008 so too did professional golf in China.

2008 saw the demise of the Beijing Open, the BMW Asian Open (a European and Asian Tour event that had been running since 2001 and boasted winners such as Darren Clarke, Ernie Els and Padraig Harrington), the Grand China LPGA Tournament and the Challenge Tours Qingdao Golf Open.

It seems that golf and the markets are just as connected in golf's newest playground as they have been for more than a century in the US and Europe. Unfortunately it appears that the relationship can at times become too close in China as well.

Corruption does not only appear through financial crisis, although that is the way it appears when one looks back historically. It was during the Great Depression, in the wake of the 1929 crash, that many fraud and corruption cases were pursued, notably of Richard Whitney, the former president of the New York Stock Exchange and Samuel Insull, the utility tycoon – and it was in the wake of the Dot Com bust in the early 2000s that cases such as Enron, Worldcom and Tyco came to light. Corruption is in fact ever present, it is just that when markets are rising and everyone is getting richer, not many questions are being asked. This all changes when the inevitable bust comes. It is then that frauds such as Madoff's Ponzi scheme unravel, and it also through the bust that someone has to be blamed and more challenging and probing questions are asked.

Golf has obviously not been the cause or to blame for any of the corporate malfeasance and scams that have been seen over the years, however, the fact that it has often been "in the vicinity at the time" is intriguing and it is more than mere coincidence. Just as corruption is always found eventually when there are large sums of money involved, so too it seems is golf. Whether it is in business, the stock market or investing in general, the relationship between the two "great games" is close, and sometimes it just gets too close.

Above: 1977 British Open, Tom Watson and Jack Nicklaus embrace after tournament on Sunday at Turnberry GC, Ailsa. (Photo by Stephen Green-Armytage/Sports Illustrated/Getty Images)

Team Europe captain Seve Ballesteros (right) celebrating with Miguel Angel Jimenez (left) during the Ryder Cup matches at Valderrama Golf Club, Sotogrande, Spain, 28th September 1997.

(Photo by Andrew Redington/Getty Images)

STEALTH: Will This Bird Fly?

DECEMBER 5, 1988

$2.00

TIME

A Game of Greed

This man could
pocket $100 million
from the largest
corporate takeover
in history. Has
the buyout craze
gone too far?

RJR Nabisco's
Ross Johnson

Above: James Cayne, former chairman and CEO of Bear
Stearns, is sworn in prior to testifying before the Financial
Crisis Inquiry Commission on Capitol Hill May 5, 2010 in
Washington, DC. The Commission held a public hearing
on 'The Shadow Banking System,' the system of bank-like
financial institutions and markets operating outside of the
regulatory structure for traditional banking activities.
(Photo by Win McNamee/Getty Images)

Above: Beth Daniel the USA team captain (left) and her assistant captain Meg Mallon (centre) with John Solheim, son of the late Karsten Solheim, president and CEO of the Karsten Manufacturing Company, owners of the Ping golf company during the Saturday morning fourball matches at the 2009 Solheim Cup Matches, at the Rich Harvest Farms Golf Club on August 22, 2009 in Ilinois *(Photo by David Cannon/Getty Images)*

Left: Stan O'Neal, former chairman, chief executive and president of Merrill Lynch. *(Photo by Joe Raedle/Getty Images)*

Above: Tiger Woods stands with runner-up Rocco Mediate after winning on the first sudden death playoff hole during the playoff round of the 108th U.S. Open at the Torrey Pines Golf Course on June 16, 2008 in San Diego, California. *(Photo by Ross Kinnaird/Getty Images)*

Left: "Know someone that got burned by sleazy Madoff? Give them the Madoff Golf balls for them to take their frustration out on. Great idea by some guy that is going to make a quick million, found at SleazeBalls.net." *(Image from www.sleazeballs.com)*

Right: Warren Buffett, chairman of Berkshire Hathaway, Inc., plays bridge with Berkshire Hathaway shareholders Sunday, May 1, 2005 in Omaha, Nebraska. *(Photo by Eric Francis/Bloomberg via Getty Images)*

The European Ryder Cup team celebrate with the trophy after the Singles Matches for The 39th Ryder Cup at Medinah Country Club on September 30, 2012 in Medinah, Illinois.
(Photo by Ross Kinnaird/Getty Images)

Ian Poulter of England celebrates with the Ryder Cup after the Singles Matches for The 39th Ryder Cup at Medinah Country Club on September 30, 2012 in Medinah, Illinois.
(Photo by Ross Kinnaird/Getty Images)

CHAPTER EIGHT
Why play either game? Who can win? Who can be great and what is the price?

"Investing is simple, but not easy." Warren Buffett
"Golf is deceptively simple and endlessly complicated." Arnold Palmer

The answer to the first question in the title of this chapter is probably the same for both "great games" primarily because they both share so many vitally important and largely attractive characteristics. Both "great games" are vastly multi-faceted and complex, and neither can ever be totally mastered nor conquered and as such they are both immensely humbling. Both also require time, no-one ever stops learning about the game, and themselves, and both require patience and discipline. These sentiments were captured in comments from the late and great, Severiano Ballesteros who in an interview with the *Daily Telegraph* summed up just what kept his passion for golf alive, and why he kept playing, long after his very best playing days were behind him.

"Golf is a game that makes you humble, and the biggest thing of all is that it needs patience. It is the best education for life of any game I know, and it makes you become an addict."

Just as either game can be described as both simple and complicated (as captured in the quotes at the top of this chapter), the comments from Seve can equally be applied to the "great game" of investing. Investing is frequently humiliating and no matter whether one is a frequent trader or a long-term investor, success requires a great deal of patience. It is probably because of these characteristics, and the underlying complexity of both activities, that both can become, as Seve points out, addictive. Just as great self-discipline is required if one is to succeed in either game so too is great discipline required to avoid the destructive path of addiction.

Both games are also intellectually challenging, not necessarily in an academic way but certainly both are mind games. In investing this is obvious – however, it is also the case in golf. As the great Bobby Jones famously put it: "Golf is a game that is played on a five inch course – the distance between your ears."

That all of these characteristics are shared by the two "great games" go some way to explaining the similarities of the two activities and also some way in answering the first question, "Why play either game?" But naturally there are many other answers. When it comes to golf the answers could include the appeal of the challenge and for the love and thrill of the game, some may be attracted by the opportunity the game offers to gain some social status and the opportunity to exercise gently in the outdoors whereas others may see it as a route to riches. All of these are valid reason for playing golf and all but the outdoor exercise can equally be applied to investing.

It is also the case that all participants in both endeavours continually strive to improve and do better. This is obvious in investing – everyone would like to lose less often and make more money more often, but in golf some might argue that this is a debateable aspect to golf's enduring appeal. However, support to this contention was provided in a beautifully written foreword to Ben Hogan's timeless book, *The Modern Fundamentals of Golf*. Published in 1957 the foreword was written by Sidney L James, then the managing editor of *Sports Illustrated* that had serialised the book.

James begins the foreword:

The yearning to play a better game of golf is a national mania in America. No man who golfs is so stubborn, so conceited, so arrogant or so accomplished that he is not constantly striving to improve his score. He may not admit this to others. He may pretend that mediocrity is enough for him. ('I shoot in the 90s and I have a lot of fun. That's good enough for me.')

This man is telling a white lie and he knows it. He wants desperately to break 90 and when he does, he will want just as desperately to break 80. Let him shoot in the high 70s and he will have but one dream: par or better.

He went on to write:

The golfer truly believes in long engagements. He courts a mistress as fickle as she is bewitching. She leads him on with little favours that fill him with hopes of conquest.

Investors court a very similar and bewitching mistress that often offers initial encouragement before delivering a far more destructive disappointment.

James writes later:

But the game, the bewitcher, will take care of him. At the moment when his confidence is highest, his happiness indescribable, she will let him have it. He will slice his drive, he will blunder his way back on to the fairway and into a trap, he will four putt the green. He will be chastened. He will know humility again.

Humility — that is the magic word. Golf is man's most humbling diversion. It may be for that reason alone, the greatest game he has ever devised. No man — champion, top professional or President of the United States — ever reaches that point at which he can say: I have learned the secret, I have conquered the bewitcher.

So many of these points, so lyrically made by James, about the appeal, attraction and frustration of golf, could be applied to investing, just as with Seve's comments earlier. In either activity to succeed with such a "bewitching mistress" requires a number of qualities. Humility is obviously vital, there can be no room for over-confidence or arrogance, patience and persistence are also essential as are discipline and a thoughtful mind. It is therefore likely that the most successful participants in either "great game", golf or investing, will display and embody substantial quantities of many, if not all, of these characteristics or traits. However, to explore more deeply the similarities between the two "great games", it is necessary to establish and understand what true success is.

Initially, success can be seen as merely winning. There are clearly many winners each year around the world on all the various golf tours, and the level of success is greater the bigger or more prestigious the tournament. The winner of a professional tournament anywhere has achieved greater success than the winner of a monthly medal. Taking this one step further, the winner of a major has achieved greater success than either. This success, however, may be fleeting, or even possibly due to luck or good fortune.

Equally, success in investing can be seen as one good trade, or one correct market call. Either of these will be enjoyable but that moment will pass. Similarly, as in golf, fleeting success may ultimately be seen as a piece of luck rather than the work of genius.

True success requires longevity and consistency, for an individual to be considered successful or even great, there need to have been many "wins" over many years or decades.

By these measures, consistency and longevity, it can easily be argued that Jack Nicklaus and Warren Buffet are the two most successful participants in their respective fields. But do they have anything else, other than success, in common that may be the catalyst or root-cause of their indisputable success? The answer is an unequivocal "yes". **Patience, Discipline and Humility.**

JACK NICKLAUS

Jack Nicklaus is without question the greatest golfer ever. Tiger Woods clearly has the potential, and time, to win more majors than Jack ever did, and may still be on schedule to do this. Therefore, on the consistent success measure, Tiger is certainly great. But as to his longevity, only time will tell. Jack won his first major in his first season as a professional aged 22, Tiger also won in his first full season and was still only 21, but Jack won his last major, on the regular tour as opposed to the senior tour, aged 46.

Tiger may once more dominate the way he has, and may ultimately win more majors over a greater period of time than Jack. However, we won't know that for another ten years or so. So at least for now, it is incontrovertible that Jack Nicklaus achieved greater true success in his career than Tiger has to date.

The other contenders for being the greatest golfers of all time, on the longevity and consistency of winning measures, are Gary Player and Bobby Jones. Player certainly won tournaments and majors over a very long period and his dedication to fitness and single mindedness have been an inspiration to millions. He is one of only five players to have won the modern Grand Slam of golf, along with Nicklaus, Sarazen, Hogan and Tiger Woods. Like Nicklaus, Player won majors over the course of three decades, and his final major, like Nicklaus, was the Masters won when in his forties. So he has without a doubt been truly successful, and may have overcome far more to achieve what he has. However, the stark facts are that Jack won many more majors, twice as many in fact.

Over the years many comparisons have been made between Bobby Jones, and what he achieved as an amateur, and Jack Nicklaus' career. These comparisons are very hard as, unlike the more recent Tiger to Nicklaus comparisons, the world was quite different when both played. When Jones was dominating the fairways, professional golf, while not quite in its infancy, was not the highly respected and highly rewarded activity it is now or when Jack was playing. Nonetheless, Bobby Jones has a rightful claim to be considered the greatest. He won a higher percentage of events entered, particularly majors, than anyone else ever has or is likely to. In addition, of course, he achieved the original Grand Slam of golf – winning the US and British Opens and Amateur Championships in a single year – an achievement that, given the changes in the game over the eighty years since and the huge rewards available for professionals, is unlikely to ever be repeated.

What Bobby Jones lacked though was the longevity that Player and Nicklaus almost uniquely displayed. He retired at his peak aged twenty-eight, something that should always be admired. But his dominance barely spanned one decade.

So Jack Nicklaus can justifiably be considered the greatest golfer ever. As Lee Trevino, his close rival through much of his career, neatly summarises:

"If Nicklaus had the equipment we have today, he would have won 40 majors. Tiger needs about four rivals, like Jack had, to say he's the best."

What made Jack so great and what kept him going for so long?

Jack Nicklaus' upbringing was middle-class and comfortable, quite a contrast to that of many of the professionals that had been dominant a generation earlier. Golf was not a means to make a living, rather it appears to have been the natural path to follow for someone with his phenomenal ability. That ability had been readily apparent in his winning of two US amateur titles along with his close challenge, when still an amateur, for the US Open title in 1960. That he should become a professional golfer was to be expected, it was a natural step. What was not clear at the time was that he was destined to become the greatest of all time, and in so doing would topple the world's favourite golfer, Arnold Palmer.

When Jack started as a professional the money was good, but not sensational. There was nothing like the corporate involvement with sponsorship and advertising that modern players have to cope with and benefit from.

Jack's career certainly had its ups and downs, both on and off the golf course. However, what continued to drive and motivate Jack long after he had achieved financial security, and even after securing a place in the record books as one of the best ever, is the real focus of this chapter.

It has never appeared to be financial goals that drove Nicklaus, unlike some other champions.

When Tony Jacklin, a working class boy from a depressed area of England, was taken under the wing of Mark McCormack's IMG golf management in addition to stating that he wanted to be the 'best golfer in the world' and to 'win all the majors' he telling commented that he 'wanted to be a millionaire'. Liz Kahn in *Tony Jacklin, The Price of Success* quotes Mark McCormack:

Motivation is the real factor. That can be the desire to reach another plateau of accomplishment or the desire to earn more money. But you have to maintain the same killer instinct you had when you were without money.

Undoubtedly after winning both the British and US Opens within one year, and later becoming a great Ryder Cup captain, Jacklin, with the help of McCormack, would have attained a level of financial security. However, McCormack's comments highlight that achieving financial goals may have lessened Jacklin's motivation to be the 'best golfer in the world'.

It is understandable that if anyone's goal is primarily financial then it may be hard to find the drive to go further once the finances are taken care of. It could also be said that it is an all too common human tendency to become comfortable and even lazy if one is over paid. Those that achieve true greatness do not succumb to this. Jack Nicklaus never got lazy and must have been focused on something other than financial rewards.

It is clear that Jack was, and is, not only hugely competitive, but also a modest man that has great respect for the disciplines and history of his chosen sport. This was never more apparent than in the British Open at Turnberry in 1977, the memorable Open that became known as "The Duel in the Sun".

Jack Nicklaus never got lazy and must have been focused on something other than financial rewards.

By then, sixteen years into his professional career, Jack was at the height of his powers. He'd already won fourteen professional majors and both the Vardon trophy for scoring average and topped the US money list eight times. Official world rankings did not exist back then but the unofficial forerunner to those rankings, compiled by the Mark McCormack Organisation and published in their *World of Professional Golf Annual* each year from 1968 through to 1985, did and Jack Nicklaus was rated number one in the world for the first ten years of those rankings. It would have been a tough argument for anyone to claim in the summer of 1977 that anyone other than Jack Nicklaus was the best golfer in the world.

Over the previous few years, several players had been heralded as "the next Jack Nicklaus", but most found the weight of such expectations too great. One who seemed a real pretender to Jack's throne was Tom Watson. A fresh-faced Kansan, Tom had won the British Open in a playoff two years earlier against Australian Jack Newton, and just a few months before the 1977 Open had hung on to beat a charging Jack Nicklaus to win the Masters title at Augusta.

The British Open of 1977 was to turn into one of the all time great golfing duels, and possibly one of sport's all time great battles. It was also to be seen, at least at the time, as possibly the moment when the next Jack Nicklaus had been found.

Over the first three days of the Championship it became clear that it was a two-horse race as both Watson and Nicklaus matched each other's daily scores. At the start of the final round, they were three strokes clear of the field, and were well on the way to rewriting the Open's scoring record book. The battle lines had been drawn. The day was going to be a day for all golf fans to remember as the pair threw everything they had at each other. As they approached the final tee, it was Watson who held the narrowest of leads, one stroke.

Watson, with the honour, played an iron into the perfect position, within easy reach of the green. The pressure was all on Nicklaus. He elected to take a driver, a club that by his standards he had been struggling with all week. It slipped to the right into long grass, frighteningly close to an area of gorse bushes. The Championship seemed lost, particularly after Watson hit a seven iron to only a few feet from the hole. But Nicklaus did not concede. Out of a lie that appeared impossible, he summoned every ounce of strength in his body and launched the ball towards the green.

It was a stroke of little grace but of enormous determination and power. At the time Peter Alliss commentating, for the BBC, described it as "the most animalistic shot he had ever seen". Few, if any players could have played that shot under any circumstances, and only a great champion, possibly only the greatest champion ever, could have executed that shot at that time.

The ball came to rest on the green, but was about as far from the hole as it was possible to be and still be on the green. Nicklaus' cause still seemed lost, one shot behind and still a long way from the hole. But Nicklaus did not concede. After stalking the putt from every angle and standing over the ball for what seemed like an age, he finally stroked it. Few could believe what happened next — after rolling for seconds the ball finally fell into the hole, right in front of Watson, for the most improbable final-hole birdie in major championship history.

The Championship was not yet over, Nicklaus had made sure of that. From having had a fairly simple putt for victory Watson now faced a real pressure putt, the hole must have appeared to shrink from its regulation 4¼ inches to a size that would barely fit the ball.

But Watson and his caddie, Alfie Fyles, had both anticipated that Nicklaus would sink the putt. Rising to the challenge, as he had throughout the Championship, Watson sank his putt. The thrill for Watson must have been almost as great as the relief. If Nicklaus had been disappointed when Watson's ball fell, it would have been understandable. If he was, it was impossible to tell.

Thirty-two years later, with the Open returning to Turnberry, Tom Watson recounted his memory of the last moments of his epic duel with Nicklaus in an interview with *The Observer* newspaper:

Jack was the most gracious competitor I've ever seen in defeat. I've never seen anybody so able to take defeat and give credit to the other player even though he is hurting so much inside. And he did that when we walked off that green. He put his arm round me and just about broke my neck, he squeezed me so hard. He said: 'Tom, I gave it my best shot but it wasn't good enough. Congratulations.'

The embrace he gave Watson after his ball fell in was more that of a proud father than a vanquished opponent. It was one of the most endearing displays of sportsmanship ever by a champion in any sport.

Frequently sportsmen are comforted in defeat, or rationalise the pain, by the idea that they should learn something from it. In the 1977 British Open, Jack Nicklaus may have learnt something, although it appeared he already knew whatever it was he should learn. The world, however, learnt a lot about Jack Nicklaus. They learnt of his humility, modesty, pride and his unquestionable respect for the sport and for his fellow competitors.

All these qualities seem integral to Nicklaus' enduring success and may provide some insight into what determines greatness in fields other than golf.

Measuring the greatness of an investor is far harder than measuring that of a golfer. There are no investing world championships, or major tournaments. However, in thinking of the qualities of longevity and consistency used to compare golfing champions, there is one name that seems head and shoulders above all others – Warren Buffett.

WARREN BUFFET

From a longevity standpoint, few investors can compare with Warren Buffet. While he may have only achieved legendary status in the relatively recent past, he has been a consistently successful investor for more than half a century. Given that few individuals in the world have achieved greater wealth in any activity, it is certainly fair to say that he has been successful and can be considered one of the greatest, if not the greatest, investor of all time. What is clear is that what drives Warren Buffett is not money – if money was all he was interested in he would have retired long ago. He obviously has an insatiable appetite to solve the challenge that investing presents, he is deeply passionate about investing and exudes enthusiasm for it above almost anything else except perhaps bridge.

Anyone who studies any of the myriad of books about Warren Buffett (there were apparently almost fifty books in print with his name in the title in 2008 according to USA Today), hears him interviewed or reads his now legendary annual letter to Berkshire Hathaway shareholders, will rapidly appreciate that those three essential qualities – humility, patience and discipline – that Jack Nicklaus displayed in his golfing career over many decades, Warren Buffett has also displayed in his investing over an even longer period.

It is worthwhile reviewing Buffett's career, from its earliest days, to observe just how evident these characteristics are.

Buffett was born in 1930, right at the start of the Great Depression, although, like Nicklaus, Buffett had a comfortable childhood. His work ethic, discipline and interest in investing all displayed themselves at a young age. When aged just ten he made a point of visiting the New York Stock Exchange when in the city and at age eleven he bought his first shares. As a young teenager he was filing his own tax returns and claimed a $35 deduction for the use of his bicycle and wristwatch on his paper round. He graduated from high school in 1947 and his senior year book reads "likes math, a future stock broker".

After high school he studied at Wharton Business School and then at the University of Nebraska where he graduated aged just nineteen with a degree in Business Administration. From there he attended Columbia Business School with the aim of studying under Benjamin Graham, the author, along with David Dodd, of *The Intelligent Investor*. Reputedly, even at a relatively young age, this now widely-followed textbook was one of Buffett's favourite books. By the time he was twenty he had saved almost $10,000, a very large sum for such a young man back in 1950. This work ethic, thrift and disciplined behaviour was to become a hallmark of the Warren Buffett that the world would eventually become so familiar with several decades later.

After working in the investment industry for various firms, including that of his former teacher Ben Graham, through the early 1950s Buffett had by 1956 accumulated personal savings of $174,000, he had also married and had two children. That year he went out on his own and set up his first investment partnership in Omaha, Nebraska, and the following year he purchased his first home, a five bedroom house costing $31,500 in which he still lives.

Much of his investment style and beliefs were undoubtedly formed at a very early age and were clearly shaped and refined by his time with Ben Graham. They served him well through his early career and investment partnerships and are broadly unchanged to this day. Warren Buffett first became a millionaire aged just thirty-two in 1962, after only five years of working for himself. Over the next three years he started to acquire shares in Berkshire Hathaway, a New England textile company, for a price that was less than the company's working capital. He soon took control of the company and from 1966 Berkshire Hathaway began to emerge as Buffett's ultimate investment vehicle as he began to unwind all other investment partnerships.

Throughout the 1970s Buffett's investment approach never deviated, despite some extremely volatile markets, and by 1979 his personal net worth had risen to $620 million. This placed him, for the first time, on Forbes list of the 400 wealthiest Americans.

The 1980s were similarly rewarding to Buffett's highly disciplined investment approach and by 1990 he had become a billionaire. While his trend to ever greater wealth continued Buffett remained the modest, some would say humble, individual that he always was. He continued to receive a very modest salary from Berkshire Hathaway and continued to live the same life he always had in his hometown of Omaha, Nebraska in his original home purchased in the late 1950s. As the 1990s continued onwards this behaviour was a world apart from that of some of the newly minted billionaires whose fortunes had seemingly miraculously appeared almost overnight as stock markets, particularly those focused on technology companies rocketed higher.

It was through this period of the booming 1990s that Buffett's discipline, self-belief and modesty were displayed for all to see.

As the decade of the 1990s was drawing to a close questions as to Buffett's investment acumen were being asked throughout the media. Respected business weekly, *Barron's*, ran the cover story in their final issue of 1999:

What's Wrong, Warren?
Berkshire Hathaway may experience its first annual stock-price
decline since 1990, hurt in part by Chief Executive
Warren Buffett's distaste for tech stocks. His commitment and
energy are unflagging, but the question is inevitable:
Who will – who can – succeed him?

The article went on to point out just how poorly Buffett's investment vehicle, Berkshire Hathaway, had done over the prior year and half, a period when most stocks, and particularly technology stocks, were booming. But even against the broader market and other more staid "blue chip" companies Berkshire Hathaway was struggling as the chart below from *Barron's* illustrated.

FALLING BEHIND

With its decline in 1999, Berkshire's class A stock now is trailing the S&P 500 index over the past five years. Berkshire also is lagging General Electric and insurance giant American International Group. Will the highly competitive Buffett bounce back?

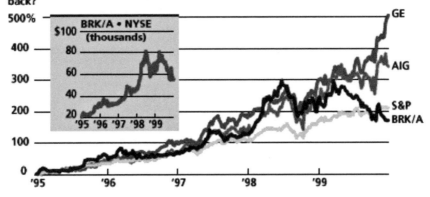

The *Barron's* article was gentle compared to some that appeared at the time but none of this changed the way Buffett invested. Going against what seemed to be a runaway train, where money could seemingly be made easily, is difficult for most individuals. It requires immense discipline and self-belief not to simply go along with the crowd, even just a little, but Buffett never did this and eventually he was vindicated.

The *Barron's* cover story in many ways could not have been better timed – it captured the peak of derision that Buffett was facing and virtually coincided with the crescendo of an historic bull market. The Dow Jones Industrial Average peaked almost simultaneously as the article appeared – and less than four years later, with the technology bubble having well and truly burst, the Dow was down about twenty percent while Berkshire Hathaway over the same period was up more than fifty percent. Seven years later the difference in performance between Buffett and the market was even starker – the Dow in late 2007 was only about twenty percent higher than it had been at its late 1999 peak, while Berkshire Hathaway had risen more than one hundred and seventy percent.

It seems that, contrary to the *Barron's* headline, there was nothing "wrong with Warren" he was merely following his highly disciplined approach to investing, one that cared little if anything about what others may believe to be the right way to invest at any time. He was also displaying his seemingly inexhaustible patience. Very few would have had the intestinal fortitude to go against the then prevailing conventional wisdom for so long, but then as Warren Buffett has frequently been quoted as saying, his favourite holding period for an investment is forever, and he wouldn't mind if the stock exchange closed for five years after he bought a share. Such discipline and patience, along with humility, are shared by all great investors, just as it seems they are shared by all great golfers.

Such discipline and patience, along with humility, are shared by all great investors, just as it seems they are shared by all great golfers.

Being a great golfer, and embodying all these characteristics, does not however ensure that one will be a great investor, just as being a great investor does not guarantee success on the golf course. Warren Buffett, it was reported by CNN, was a golf fanatic in his youth, but in a call with CNN journalist Patricia Sellers in 2011 he reported that "lucky to break 100 would be a very generous appraisal of my current abilities". Being in his eighties now this is understandable, however, there is a fascinating, and slightly obscure, connection between Warren Buffett and one of the most important golfing events in the world, the Ryder Cup, and that is through his other passion – bridge. Warren Buffet was an early supporter of the biennial bridge competition between Europe and the US that is modelled on the Ryder Cup and staged immediately prior to the Ryder Cup in the same region of either the US or Europe. The Buffett Cup has been competed for since 2006.

THE RYDER AND BUFFETT CUPS

Just as there exists a parallel between the investment markets of the US and Europe and either side's performance in the Ryder Cup an equally valuable indicator, albeit in reverse, may be emerging in the still young Buffett Cup.

The Ryder Cup was born during the 1920s, a period of rampant optimism that culminated in a stock market boom followed by a desperate crash and the Great Depression. Throughout that pre-Second World War period the fortunes of golf closely followed the fortunes of the stock market and the relative performance of either side of the Atlantic's stock markets were mirrored in the results of the Ryder Cup. Unlike professional golf, however, that struggled through the nineteen thirties, bridge did not, in fact it boomed. The heyday of bridge as a widely followed competitive event was the 1930s and in 1938 three books on bridge – *Complete Contract Bridge, Culbertson's Own New Contract Bridge and Five Suit Bridge* – made the *New York Times* best seller list.

During the 1930s regular trans-Atlantic bridge challenges were held and it is reported that interest in these events was so high that they frequently dominated the front pages of the newspapers on both sides of the Atlantic. Over the subsequent decades competitive bridge continued to flourish, however, the level of public interest that was evident in the 1930s has not been seen again, although that may now be changing thanks largely to Warren Buffett.

Perhaps inspired by the enormous event that the Ryder Cup had become, a number of prominent bridge players from both sides of the Atlantic began discussions about staging a Europe versus America bridge challenge. When it became known that the 2006 Ryder Cup was going to be held in Ireland plans were laid to hold a trans-Atlantic challenge match, in Ireland, immediately prior to the Ryder Cup at the K Club with a head-to-head format as close to that of the Ryder Cup as possible. Prior to that first staging of the challenge match, Warren Buffett, whose enthusiasm and playing ability are substantially higher in bridge than golf, lent his support to the project. The Buffett Cup was born.

The inaugural event was held in Dublin and the thirteen-person American team defeated the Europeans. A few days later this result was avenged on the golf course when the Europeans emerged triumphant and retained the Ryder Cup. Two years later, in Kentucky, it was the Europeans that struck the first blow by winning the Buffett Cup, but again the result was reversed on the golf course when the Americans achieved only their second win in the last seven encounters and their most comfortable win for decades.

After the first two Buffett Cup competitions a trend was beginning to emerge. Unlike the Ryder Cup, that throughout its history has reflected the ebb and flow of the respective team's home stock markets – it appeared that the Buffett Cup was an inverse reflection of relative stock market performance. For some reason it seems that whichever side of the Atlantic's stock market was faring the worst or the most depressed, the better their bridge players did!

Why this should be is impossible to say and two results only is far from confirmation of a relationship, but the fact that bridge did so well during the Great Depression, a time when most other pastimes struggled, is intriguing and any intrigue surrounding this seemingly reverse relationship was enhanced by the 2010 Buffett and Ryder Cups.

The 2010 Ryder Cup, played over the purpose-built Ryder Cup course at Celtic Manor, witnessed yet another close battle but ultimately the Europeans prevailed by the narrowest of margins. That year the markets of Europe and the US had given no indication as to which side would win – they had delivered the exact same returns over the preceding two years, so a closely fought match may have been inevitable. The Buffett Cup, on the other hand, had been of value to any one hoping to pick the winning Ryder Cup team. The Buffett Cup was held in nearby Cardiff, and the Americans regained the trophy but just as in both prior Buffett Cups the victor's celebrations did not last through the weekend as the winning bridge team witnessed their countrymen lose the Ryder Cup.

YOU CAN'T BUY A GAME!

Great golfers and great investors do what they do because they love it, and because they love what they do they apply themselves in an extremely dedicated and disciplined fashion. As a result their achievements ultimately set them apart from their peers, but that was not their goal it was merely an outcome, and successful careers in both golf and investing have generally been characterised more by humility than arrogance. Great wealth, particularly over the last forty or fifty years, has also been an outcome of success in either field, but while a number can be put on the wealth that the successful achieve a price cannot be attached to achieving that success. As Sam Snead famously quipped many years ago: "You can't go into a shop and buy a good game of golf."

The same can be said of investing, success cannot be bought. Nonetheless, in both "great games" most participants would dearly love to be able to "buy a game".

Both investing and golf are absorbing, frustrating and can become almost addictive. They are also hard and are never totally mastered by anyone, at least not for long, and the moment anyone thinks that they may have cracked "it" rapid disappointment is never far away.

Given that both golf and investing share these common characteristics it is understandable that most investors and golfers want to get better at their chosen activity and many are tempted to believe that they can buy a game. It is therefore reasonable to explore the question of whether, with the application of modern technology, it is possible to do just that. There is certainly a very large industry, made up of fund managers, investment advisers, computer programmers, stockbrokers and golf equipment manufacturers and teachers, who would have us believe that better results are virtually certain if only we bought this or paid for a series of those. Undoubtedly when used the right way many of these devices or tips may result in improvement, but it's often the "using the right way" that is hard.

Technology has certainly changed both investing and golf over the past hundred years and in some ways has made both look like less of the art they once were and possibly look more like a science.

In investing, technology has certainly sped things up, information is far more readily available and transactions are almost immediate. Computer technology and the internet have allowed anyone to monitor virtually any investment market anywhere in the world twenty-four hours a day, and there is a proliferation of so called "systems" that will supposedly tell an investor or day trader when they should buy and when they should sell. It would be nice if investing could be made easy, but unfortunately if it were made easy, and the next twist or turn in a market was obvious to everyone, then markets would never move – everyone would be waiting for the same next signal and everyone would be on the same side of a trade that therefore couldn't take place.

However, neither the application of technology nor money will guarantee investment success. Technology has certainly made investing more democratic, in that everyone has similar access to most information and opportunities, however, everyone can't be a winner. The best investors are still the best investors probably because they have a deep and passionate understanding and feeling for investing. Investing is still an art, not a science, and like any art improvement only comes from diligent practice, study and experience, no matter how much natural talent one may have. Gary Player said, "You must work very hard to be a natural golfer," the same is true of investing.

Golf has also changed dramatically at the hands of technology. At the turn of the last century the ball had improved from being one of leather stuffed with feathers to a hard lump of solid rubber, the "guttie". This allowed a fuller and harder swing to be exercised, but with that unresponsive ball and the somewhat fragile and twisty hickory shafted clubs available, a good drive, even by a strong player like J H Taylor, might only travel 200 yards.

The guttie was subsequently replaced by the wound Haskell ball and then in 1921 its size and weight was somewhat standardised.

Around this time, when rules standardising various characteristics of the ball came into being, one of the greatest steps forward in golf was made – the introduction, and subsequent legalisation, of steel shafted clubs both in the US and then in Great Britain. This step alone made golf an easier game for more players than any other single development before or since.

More recently developments have come fairly regularly and have largely been aimed at making golf easier through genuine innovation or by testing the limits of tolerances set by the sport's governing bodies.

The culmination, or at least the clear articulation, of this trend was to come with the emergence of the "Big Bertha" and Callaway Golf in 1990. The big-headed metal woods have more in common with leading edge aerospace design than the traditional image of a craftsman carving a work of art out of a solid block of persimmon. The aim of the Big Bertha's creator, Ely Callaway, was to make a hard game easier, and it certainly did that as many golfers who would never have dared to use a wooden driver rushed to buy first a Big Bertha, then a Great Big Bertha and all the high tech models that followed. The result was fantastic business for Callaway Golf and a meaningful change in the character and nature of golf.

Golf may have become more forgiving as a result of all these technological improvements, and has therefore become easier, but it has got easier for everyone. Just as most amateurs now use large headed forgiving drivers so too have professionals moved ahead. Major championships are now won, over longer but otherwise similar courses, with scores thirty or forty shots better than winning scores from a hundred years ago. The game may have been made easier and more enjoyable for more people through technology but if everyone has equal access to it then, relatively speaking, nothing has changed.

Improvement in relative terms comes through application, practice, experience and understanding. No golfer will become an automaton and no computer program will consistently beat the market. Both activities may look more scientific than before but both are still very much an art, and are arts where hard work, dedication, emotion and psychology play an enormous role in determining success or failure. Money may help keep the playing field even but neither game can be bought.

The same individuals who are the best golfers today would almost certainly have been the best golfers in an earlier age, and those greats from the past would almost certainly have been greats in the modern game. The same is true of investing. The way markets are followed may have changed, the availability of information has certainly changed, but a truly great investor now would have succeeded a century ago and those legends of investing from earlier generations would still be masters of the "art" of investing now.

CHAPTER NINE
2012 and Beyond

*"They say golf is like life, but don't believe them.
Golf is more complicated than that."* Gardner Dickinson

Throughout 2012 golf and investment markets continued to reflect the majority of the relationships that have been outlined in *Bulls, Birdies, Bogeys and Bears*. The US stock market spent the majority of the year rising and recorded its highest levels since early 2008. Consistent with the observations made in chapter four "The Gender Gap" this generally positive stock market backdrop has not been conducive to the "gap" closing, in fact it widened quite dramatically. With the majority of the golf season over it is looking like the leading male professional will win more than three times the total of the leading female golfer. This is not as extreme a gap as has been seen at long term peaks in the market but it is a world apart from the approaches to parity that were seen in the 80s and early 90s.

The male money winner's total is also reflective of where markets have been in 2012 compared to prior years. The leading male golfer looks set to comfortably exceed Matt Kuchar's total of less than $5 million won in 2010 but will fall along way short of the almost $11 million that Tiger Woods accumulated in 2007, the year most developed stock markets hit their all time highs. Looking forward it seems that markets will need to hit a substantial new all time high sometime in the coming years if the leading professional golfer is to see his winnings meaningfully exceed the $10 million mark that was first hit twelve years ago. Alternatively, if markets were to drop into another bear market, as they have twice over the last twelve years, male professional golf would almost certainly struggle, as it did through those earlier periods, and the gender gap might narrow again.

A number of other relationships, and their developments through 2012, warrant a little closer examination. The first is the relative performance of one region's golfers compared to another's and whether this has continued to correlate with the respective region's stock market returns over the very recent past. The second is how Tiger Woods has continued to reflect the performance of the stock market in an uncanny echo of Jack Nicklaus thirty-four years earlier.

In chapter three "The Ryder Cup" the long-term relationship between the performance of either side of the Atlantic's professional golfers and the returns of their respective stock markets was explored in some depth. The chapter concluded that, rather than the relationship being merely a coincident reflection of the wider ebb and flow of aggregate social mood, there was actually some predictive value in the stock market when it came to Ryder Cup results, particularly since the early 1980s. Broadly speaking there has only been one Ryder Cup match since then when the markets "got it wrong" – the epic battle in 1997 when Europe were led by the legendary Severiano Ballesteros, Seve, who loved the challenge of the Ryder Cup and proved such a charismatic leader. Whether his long time Ryder Cup partner and protégé, Jose Maria Olazabal, could repeat this feat and, like Seve, reverse what the markets indicated would be a comfortable win for the US was one of the most eagerly awaited questions as the Ryder Cup approached and European markets continued to struggle while the US markets rose.

Before reviewing the now historic events at Medinah in late September of 2012, another international stock market comparison, and its relationship to golf, is worthy of review as throughout 2012 the closeness of the great games' relationship continued to be confirmed much to the surprise, and disappointment, of investors.

THE EMERGING MARKETS AND 2012

A widely held view among many investment commentators, for much of the last decade, has been that a long-term transition has been unfolding within global investment markets. A transition that would see the developed markets, particularly of the United States and of "Old" Europe, yield their position of long-term market capitalisation dominance to the rapidly growing and demographically strong emerging markets. Certainly through the bull market, that began in the immediate aftermath of the collapse in technology, media and telecoms stocks, this appeared to be the case. That collapse saw the technology dominated US NASDAQ index down by almost eighty percent and the broader averages, in both the US and Europe, down by almost half at their low point in late 2002 to early 2003.

A new bull market did begin but the real action was in those widely touted emerging markets. One clear example was Korea where the KOSPI Index increased more than fourfold from early 2003 through to late 2007, twice the appreciation that the S&P 500 managed to produce over the same period. Another even more dramatic example of the strength in the bull market of the early to mid 2000s was seen in India, one of the so called BRIC (Brazil, Russia, India and China) countries. As the popularity of investing in emerging markets grew, and the memory of the Asian crisis and Russian default in the second half of the 1990s faded, investors rushed into the Indian market. This flurry of excitement over the prospects for India produced a more than seven fold increase in the SENSEX Index up to its peak as 2007 ended. What made this surge even more dramatic was that it came on the heels of more than a decade of a frustratingly volatile but sideways-moving market. The emergence of India as an investment opportunity in the early 2000s coincided with the emergence of India as a golfing nation.

Golf and India have a long and distinguished history. The first golf club to be formed outside of the British Isles was the Royal Calcutta Golf Club in 1829 meaning that golf was played on the Indian sub-continent almost sixty years before the first courses opened in the United States. While more clubs did follow Royal Calcutta, with Royal Bombay in 1842, Bangalore in 1876 and Shilong in 1886, golf remained a minority sport, but by the 2000s this was finally starting to change. By the late 2000s there were more than 160 golf courses in

India but they were still largely the preserve of the wealthy. However, coincident with the SENSEX booming, a succession of young Indian professionals rocketed onto the professional golf scene.

Most prominent among this new group of professionals was Jeev Milka Singh. He was the first Indian golfer to become a member of the European tour and enjoyed his most successful year by far in 2006. With four wins worldwide that year he won the Asian order of merit and his win in the European season-ending Volvo Masters gave him a final ranking of 16th in Europe. The win in the Volvo Masters also pushed his world ranking up to 37th, it came on the same day as India's cricketers lost a test and, as if to illustrate golf's growing importance, resulted in one newspaper headlining with, "Indian team losses but Jeev makes up for us". Later that year Jeev was named Indian Sportsman of the Year and was then awarded India's second highest civilian honour.

The Indian surge was far from a one man show – Arjun Atwal was the first Indian to achieve membership of the US PGA Tour in 2004, was the first Indian to win a European tour event in 2002 and in 2003 became the first player to win more than US$1 million in a season on the Asian Tour. Also in 2002 Jyonti Randhawa became the first Indian to win the Asian order of merit, he then became a full member of the European Tour.

Since that bull market of the mid 2000s, when the emerging markets boomed and their golfers flourished, markets obviously collapsed during the Global Financial Crisis and, not surprisingly, those markets that had rallied the most tended to suffer the largest falls. The Indian SENSEX fell by more than sixty percent and the Korean KOSPI by almost sixty percent. What has been more interesting has been watching the progress, or lack of, of both emerging markets and their golfers through much of 2012.

Korea is the emerging market that has so far produced the most world class male professional golfers who, since the Global Financial Crisis ran its course, have delivered two notable golfing triumphs. The first was in August 2009, almost exactly six months after the major markets of the world finally hit bottom, when Y E Yang produced one of golf's most dramatic surprises in years. After shooting a best of the day third round 67 Yang still trailed Tiger Woods by two strokes going into the last round of that year's final major, the US PGA. Expectations of a fifteenth major for Woods were justifiably high, he had never lost a major having held the fifty four hole lead. But on that Sunday in August 2009 history was made, Yang again equalled the best score of a very difficult day with a 70 while Woods fell away to a very disappointing and surprising 75 so ultimately handing Yang a comfortable three stroke victory.

Over the last two days of the 2009 US PGA the momentum had clearly been behind Yang and by August 2009 the momentum in the investment world was just as clearly behind South Korea, at least when compared to the US. By the week of the PGA the Korean market had risen close to eighty percent from its low point ten or eleven months earlier, over that same period the US market, as measured by the S&P 500, having bottomed several months later, had only risen fifteen percent.

The Korean investing momentum continued through to the next global highlight for Korean male professional golfers – the 2011 Players Championship and K J Choi's memorable victory. It marked the highpoint to date in Choi's already distinguished PGA career and may have marked the high point for male Korean golf in general. It certainly coincided almost exactly with the highpoint to-date in the Korean stock market.

When K J Choi arrived at Sawgrass for the 2011 Players Championship the KOSPI was riding a wonderfully positive wave, less than two weeks earlier it had closed at an all time high of 2228, up almost one hundred and fifty percent from its low point less than three years earlier. Over that same period the US market was only up a third of that amount.

After David Toms made a rare birdie on the seventy-second hole Choi sank his three foot par putt to ensure that there would be a playoff between him and Toms, a playoff he eventually won comfortably. It was Choi's eighth and most important victory on the PGA Tour, but since then neither he, nor any other Korean male professional, has won another PGA Tour title. In fact it seems that since Choi's Players victory Korean men's professional golf has slipped into something of a decline and over the same period the South Korean market has struggled. The KOSPI is still ten percent lower than it was when Choi last won yet the S&P 500 has continued to rise to new recovery highs.

As 2011 came to an end Korean men's professional golf was in a very healthy position on both the US Tour and in the Official World Rankings. There were four South Korean men ranked in the top fifty in the world, only the USA with eighteen, England with six and Australia with five had more. For the Koreans K J Choi led the way, ranked 15th (up from 47th a year earlier), K T Kim followed ranked 25th (up from 29th at the end of 2010), Sang-Moon Bae had risen from 149th to 30th in 2011 and the 2009 PGA champion, Y E Yang, was ranked 45th down slightly from 42nd at the end of 2010.

As the KOSPI struggled in 2012 so too did the Korean golfers – Choi fell to 38th and Moon slipped to 48th, these were the only two Koreans still in the world's top fifty, K T Kim had slumped to 68th and Y E Yang to 93rd. It seems that if Korean men's professional golf is to rise again, at least as represented in results on the US Tour and in the Official World Rankings, then the KOSPI will probably have to once again be outperforming the US market, rather than struggling as it has since Choi's Players victory. The same is almost certainly not true for Korean women.

The inverse "gender gap" relationship, discussed at length in chapter four, focused largely on the relative earnings of male professionals versus female professionals on their respective US tours. It did not look at the underlying nationality of those players involved, however, as Korean male professionals faltered through 2012 while the KOSPI has struggled, the reverse has been true for Koreans on the LPGA Tour.

The decline in performance and ranking of male Korean professionals can be traced back to KJ Choi's victory in the 2011 Players championship and the coincident peaking and reversal of the

Korean stock market while the US market continued to rise. Over that same period female Korean golfers have excelled, at least as measured in victories in the majors, particularly when compared to their American counterparts. This has been especially obvious in 2012. Of the four majors —the Kraft Nabisco Championship, the LPGA Championship, the US Women's Open and the Women's British Open, three were won by Koreans — dominance by one country in the female majors not seen since 1999 when Americans won three of the four majors. That year was a good year for the US market, but not when compared to the Korean market which almost doubled while the US S&P 500 rose less than twenty percent. 1999 was the year the Korean markets shook off the worst effects of the Asian crisis but 1998 had been miserable for Korean investors. The KOSPI hit its low, down about seventy percent over the prior two years, and bounced along at that depressed level while all that year's majors were played. In spite of this, and perversely possibly because of this, that was when female Korean golf really arrived with Se Ri Pak winning two majors. It seems that, just as in the Solheim Cup, the relative performance of one country's female golfers versus another's, is inversely related to the relative performance of their respective stock markets. The exact reverse of the pattern so clearly seen in the male sport for so long in the Ryder Cup.

Over the last half dozen years there have been four occasions where women professionals from either Korea or the US have markedly outperformed the other in terms of golfing majors, 2007, 2008, 2010 and 2012. On each occasion the country with the least successful stock market has been the most successful in terms of golf. In 2007 the markets of both countries rallied then peaked but Korea's was easily the most rewarding, the US won two majors, Korea none. 2008 was largely a reversal of 2007, both markets fell but Korea fell the most, Korea won two and the US none. 2010 was in many ways a repeat of 2007 with both markets rising but Korea rallying far more than the US, again the underperforming US won two majors to Korea's nil. Finally Korea's underperformance in 2012 has coincided with three majors while the outperforming US won none.

Among the BRIC countries only India and China have male golfers ranked in the top few hundred in the world and, like Korea, those few BRIC golfers and their markets have, in the main, disappointed in 2012. Overall the index of BRIC's markets has moved sideways in 2012, a marked underperformance of the US market. And the BRIC's index languishes at the same level as it was three years ago while the S&P 500 is up more than forty percent. China's only world-ranked golfer over the last few years has been Liang Wen Chong, he won the Chinese amateur title three years in a row from 1996 to 1998 and then turned pro in 1999. His first professional success came in the Asian and European Tours' co-sanctioned Singapore Masters in 2007. That success saw his official World Ranking climb to 86 by the end of the year. Just a year earlier he had been ranked 140th and at the end of 2005 he had been a lowly 194th on the rankings. His rise up the world rankings coincided with a marked acceleration upwards in the Chinese stock market. However, in late 2007, along with most markets in the world, the Chinese market cracked wide open and through 2008 fell by about seventy percent, Liang's world ranking fell too, he ended 2008 back down at 107th. 2009 was a much better year for the Chinese market as in less than twelve months it doubled in value, it was also a better year for Liang and his ranking recovered to 82nd as the year ended. Through the first few months of 2010 the Chinese market moved sideways before sliding into a decline from which it still, more than two years later, has not broken out of. Early 2010 was reasonable for Liang too and his ranking rose to a career high of 57th but in the second half of 2010 Liang fell into an even deeper slump than the Chinese market. By the end of the next year his ranking had fallen to a distressingly depressed 251st and the plunge continued into 2012 with him coming close to falling out of the top 500 late in the year.

For India the story has been only half as bleak as it has for China. The SENSEX index has been a disappointment in 2012, falling by about fifteen percent but their leading golfer has bucked that trend. Jeev Milka Singh has once again broken back into the world's top one hundred players, but unfortunately the story for those other players that led the vanguard of Indian golf in the early 2000s has been more reminiscent of China's Liang.

Obviously there is no tied relationship between individual players and their home country's stock market but it is certainly fascinating that there so often appears to be a connection of some kind, albeit directly for male golfers and an inverse relationship in the female sport.

While emerging markets generally, and BRIC markets in particular, have been disappointing in 2012 the same cannot be said of the US market, and coincident with the US market outperforming most other markets in the world so too have US golfers. At the end of 2011 only three Americans were ranked amongst the top ten in the world, that figure rose to five late in the 2012 season. At the same time the number ranked in the top twenty moved up from just seven to twelve and the number in the top thirty stood at sixteen, up from twelve at the beginning of the year. Such improvement in the country's golfers and the strength of the US market, particularly compared to a struggling Europe, meant that hopes were high heading into what has become one of the most watched sporting events in the world, the Ryder Cup.

THE 2012 RYDER CUP (& BUFFETT CUP)

Every two years the Ryder Cup is one of the most eagerly awaited golfing events on the sporting calendar and 2012 was no exception. Going into the event the US were favourites with the bookmakers to regain the trophy for only the third time in nineteen years and the action of the stock markets on either side of the Atlantic appeared to justify this favouritism. One, albeit substantially less proven and rational indicator, was less encouraging to the Americans – the Buffett Cup.

The first three Buffett Cups, the trans-Atlantic bridge challenge played immediately prior to the Ryder Cup, had given a perfect contrary indication as to which side would win the Ryder Cup. After just three results it may have been too early to ascribe any significance to the results and identify a trend, nonetheless, it added a little to the excitement ahead of the Ryder Cup at Medinah that the American team comfortably retained the Buffett Cup, played for the first time away from the host city of the Ryder Cup in Warren Buffett's home town of Omaha, Nebraska. If the brief history of the event was to be any sort of guide then it indicated that the Europeans should win the Ryder Cup, exactly the opposite result indicated by the return of the two side's stock markets.

Despite the euro reversing its more than one-year decline against the dollar ahead of the event, this only brought the currency back to where it had been two years earlier and so did not make up for the enormous underperformance that had been seen in European stock markets compared to the US market since the last Ryder Cup in Wales. Not only were the markets strongly favouring the Americans, so too were the bookmakers, this was eerily reminiscent of the backdrop ahead of the "Spanish Ryder Cup" at Valderrama in Spain when the charismatic Seve led Europe to an extremely unlikely victory.

Then, Tom Kite, the US Captain, had described his team as the "Dream Team" and they certainly sported substantially higher set of world rankings. The same was true, only to a slightly lesser extent, heading into the 2012 event. Both teams had four players ranked in the top ten in the world but the US had eleven ranked in the top twenty, on the European side only six were in the top twenty and three were outside the top thirty. The average ranking for America was between twelve and thirteen while for Europe it was between eighteen and nineteen. This difference may sound large but a match pitting the eighteenth and nineteenth ranked players, coincidentally both Europeans, against the twelfth and thirteenth ranked players, equally coincidentally, both Americans, would have seen Graeme McDowell and Sergio Garcia against Steve Stricker and Dustin Johnston, a far more evenly matched prospect.

While European stocks had markedly underperformed since the 2010 Ryder Cup for the three and a half months ahead of Medinah,

Europe had been the better performer, albeit from a depressed level. From the early June lows that both sides of the Atlantic recorded Europe had rallied twenty-seven percent and the US just seventeen percent. On top of this the Euro had also appreciated six percent against the dollar. Remarkably this was also a very similar relative performance to that seen in the three months ahead of Valderrama.

The opening ceremony at Medinah on the Thursday evening was accompanied by rioting in a number of European cities over the austerity measures that were being put in place. At the same time markets on both sides of the Atlantic appeared to shrug off these concerns as well as those over the so called fiscal cliff in the US and the upcoming presidential elections.

When the long-awaited match finally began on Friday 28th September the golf was accompanied by lacklustre trading in the markets on both sides of the Atlantic. European stocks fell throughout the day and the US market was never in positive territory, and with that backdrop the Americans delivered what the markets, and the bookmakers had been expecting, an early lead. The morning foursomes were shared equally with both sides winning two matches, although the American wins were more comfortable, however, the afternoon saw the Americans stamp their authority on the first day. They won three of the four matches in the afternoon fourballs to lead after the first day 5–3. Surprisingly, and disappointingly for the Americans and team captain Davis Love III in particular, Tiger Woods added no points to his already disappointing Ryder Cup record on the first day, losing his morning foursomes match on the seventeenth and the afternoon fourball on the eighteenth.

When the second day's play began on Saturday markets were obviously closed for the weekend after a disappointing week on both sides of the Atlantic. Friday's falls had brought European markets down almost five percent on the week and the weak close on Friday meant that Wall Street suffered its worst weekly fall in three months, but still a more modest decline than that of Europe, less than two percent. Even in weakness the US market was outperforming and this outperformance spread on to the fairways of Medinah.

The score sheet would report that the Saturday was almost a repeat of Friday with the home side coming out ahead with five points against the Europeans three, however, for much of the afternoon the situation looked substantially bleaker for the visitors than the score would finally show. In the morning foursomes the Americans won three matches including Bradley and Mickelson trouncing Donald and Westwood by a Ryder Cup record-equalling seven and six. The Europeans sole point coming from Justin Rose and Ian Poulter's defeat of Bubba Watson and Webb Simpson. Mid-way through the afternoon it appeared that the Americans just might get a clean sweep of the four fourball matches after Watson and Simpson comfortably clinched their match against Rose and Molinari five and four. But then, very gradually, the tide turned in Europe's favour with some inspired performances, particularly from Ian Poulter, and Europe managed to secure the last two matches, both on the final hole.

This left the USA on ten points and Europe on six leaving the Americans needing just four and a half points from the final day's singles matches to take the Ryder Cup back for only the third time since 1993, and by Saturday evening the bookmakers were favouring the Americans even more strongly, offering the extreme odds of eight to one on a European victory.

The Sunday of a Ryder Cup always seems to produce incredible theatre and 2012 at Medinah proved to be no exception to that rule, despite the apparently desperate position that the Europeans found themselves in. No visiting team had ever overcome such a large point deficit going into the final singles and the Europeans had never done so, even at home. Only at Brookline, in 1999, had Ben Crenshaw's team come back from such a seemingly insurmountable position, but then they had home soil advantage and the markets were strongly favouring a US victory.

ANOTHER "SPANISH" RYDER CUP

The only hope for Jose Maria Olazabal and his team was that somehow they were going to pull off an even more unexpected upset than the late Severiano Ballesteros had conjured up at Valderrama fifteen years earlier. Leading up to Medinah there were a number of parallels with the events leading up to the 1997 Ryder Cup but even the most ardent European supporter could not have anticipated what actually occurred on Sunday.

Almost certainly the strongest parallel was that the European captain was Seve's long time Ryder Cup partner and memories of Seve and his spirit seemed to be everywhere at Medinah. The European team bags sported Seve's famous silhouette, as did their uniforms, and on Sunday the team all played in Seve's simple outfit of dark blue with a white tee shirt. To top this off a European bookmaker had commissioned skywriting "tweets" that invoked Seve's spirit, these continued into the final day despite the efforts of an Illinois congressman to have them banned.

Seve's spirit may have been with the Europeans but they still had to win eight of the twelve matches on Sunday if they were to retain the Ryder Cup, a daunting task given that they had not won any of the four sessions on the first two days and the momentum through the majority of those two days had all been with the favourites, the Americans.

Captain Olazabal stacked his top order with his most in form players, and they delivered. In little more than an hour from twenty past two through to three thirty, first Luke Donald, followed by Paul Lawrie, Rory Mcilroy and then the hero of the first two days for Europe, Ian Poulter all won their matches. The score line then stood at ten points to both sides and the totally unexpected seemed possible. Ten minutes later Dustin Johnson defeated Nicolas Colsaerts but almost immediately Justin Rose sunk an enormous putt on the seventeenth to take the wind out of Phil Mickelson's sails and then won the final hole to once again tie the score, now at eleven points all. Over the next fifty minutes first Zach Johnson for the US won a point and then Lee Westwood for

Europe matched it and the score was still tied at twelve all. Within two minutes veteran Jim Furyk bogeyed the last, having already bogeyed the seventeenth, to hand victory to Spaniard Sergio Garcia. For the first time in the match the Europeans were ahead and within one point of retaining the trophy. A quarter of an hour later, after Jason Dufner secured victory over Peter Hanson the score was once again tied with only two matches out on the course and both those matches were also all square.

The match could not have been closer but none of the four competitors in the final two matches had won a single point over the prior two days, including the world number two, Tiger Woods.

Martin Kaymer of Germany sank a five foot putt on the last at five thirteen to defeat Steve Stricker and secure the fourteenth point for Europe, so ensuring that the trophy was at least retained by Europe, but still out on the course, playing the final hole, were Tiger Woods and Italian Francesco Molinari. Woods, having won the seventeenth, was one up and a half at the last would still have meant that the score was tied at fourteen all, but Woods, completing what was another disappointing Ryder Cup for him, missed a short putt for a par and so halved his match with the Italian and left the Europeans the most unlikely victors in Ryder Cup history, by the narrowest of margins – 14½ to 13½.

The bookmakers and the markets had got it wrong, badly wrong, just as they had in 1997. It seems that if the Europeans need to overcome the omens of the markets then they need to play the "Spanish Card". There have only ever been two Spanish Ryder Cup captains and they were both winners when the form, the bookmakers and the markets said they shouldn't be. Perhaps there is a message there for the selection of future Ryder Cup captains.

The 2012 European victory means the market's record in forecasting the Ryder Cup has slipped a little. Of the twelve matches that have had a clear result since 1983, and where the markets have given a clear signal, the markets have been right ten times. A still impressive eighty-three percent success ratio and, coincidentally, exactly the same degree of accuracy as the contrary indicator provided by the markets for the Women's Solheim Cup.

One indicator that, for whatever reason, improved its record in 2012 was the Buffett Cup. In its fourth contesting it again got the result of the main event, The Ryder Cup, totally wrong!

TIGER VERSUS JACK IN 2012

The parallels between Jack and Tiger, discussed in chapter five, continued through 2012. Tiger began the year looking to move closer to Jack's record haul of eighteen majors and despite not having won a major since 2008 the fourteen that he had already accumulated in his sixteen years on tour, left him right on schedule to at least match Jack's total. By the beginning of 1978 Jack had also won fourteen majors and had been winless in the majors over the prior two seasons.

From a stock market standpoint the two years, 1978 and 2012, despite both being more than a decade into a very long-term trading range bear market, began with quite different expectations. 1977 had been a miserable year for the market whereas 2011 had been reasonably constructive. Nonetheless, both years saw encouraging starts from the market and so too did Jack and Tiger.

In fact Jack began 1978 with a roar, a little like the markets that year. In his first five events he recorded two wins and two seconds. Undoubtedly this would have boosted his confidence ahead of that year's Masters, however, despite finishing strongly with a 69 and a 67 he finished seventh, four behind Gary Player, who closed the tournament with a 64.

His next five tournaments saw something of a slump. He missed one cut and had only two top ten finishes, and so went into the British Open at St Andrews, still chasing that elusive fifteenth major, probably with less confidence than when he arrived at Augusta. Pushing that slump in form aside Jack began with rounds of 71, 71 and 69 and he entered the final round one stroke behind the defending champion, and the man who many believed to be the "next Jack Nicklaus", Tom

Watson. Jack closed with another 69 while Watson fell away to a 76 and so Jack clinched his third British Open, his third Grand Slam and his fifteenth major. In the four remaining tournaments that Jack played in he recorded one win, two top tens and a missed cut. It had been a good year for Jack, particularly through the middle months and the same was true of the market in 1978.

For Tiger 2012 saw a marked improvement on his previous few years. He won the Arnold Palmer Bay Hill Invitational, his final event prior to the Masters, however, at Augusta rounds of 72, 75, 72, and 74 left him in a disappointing tie for fortieth, his worst finish at Augusta as a professional.

Markets had rallied in a steady but unspectacular fashion through the early months of 2012 but began to struggle in May and that correction coincided with poor finishes for Tiger in both the Wells Fargo Championship, where he missed the cut, and the Players Championship where, like at Augusta, he finished tied for fortieth.

As May ended so too did the market's setback and Tiger's fortunes also improved. He won the Memorial Tournament and four weeks later he won the AT&T National but sandwiched in between those two wins was the US Open. After leading at the halfway mark it seemed that finally Tiger was going to win major number fifteen but he faltered with closing rounds of 75 and 73 to ultimately finish outside the top twenty. Three weeks later Tiger contended at the British Open but a final round of 73, versus the eventual winner, Ernie Els' 68, left him four behind and in a tie for third. It was his best finish of the year in a major, just as Jack's British Open thirty-four years earlier was his, but now for the first time since 2001 Tiger was behind Jack's major winning pace.

In the final major of the year, the PGA, Tiger again faded in the last two rounds. After being tied for the lead at the half-way point closing rounds of 74 and 72 left him just outside the top ten and a distant eleven shots behind Rory McIlroy. That victory for Rory was his second major in two years. Whether Rory will go on to win as many majors as Jack's then young rival, Tom Watson did, or even as many as Tiger or Jack, only time will tell. At the current pace he is winning them as fast and as young as both Jack and Tiger did. What is more interesting is whether Tiger will manage to match Jack's record.

In 2012 and 1978 both Tiger and Jack enjoyed the tailwind of rising markets, both had good seasons and both won three tour events, but neither won the money title, Tiger was second and Jack was fourth. The "major" difference between them was the British Open title, the fifteenth major, which Jack won.

For the remarkable echo between Jack and Tiger, across three and a half decades, to continue Tiger needs to win at least one major in 2013, whether he will should make for fascinating viewing, as will the progress of the markets.

CONCLUSIONS AND OUTLOOK

Golf thrives during periods of improved economic activity, and so too, at least over the very long term, do stock markets. These relationships make sense, however, it would be overly simplistic to assume that there is any neat cause and effect at work between the economy, the stock market or indeed golf.

Amid the uncertainty of ever-changing and frequently volatile markets it is tempting to seek something to hang on to, something that will make "sense" of the otherwise seemingly "senseless" markets, and something that just might foretell where markets will go next, economics and economists frequently are seized upon to fill this void. This has been the case for decades and, surprisingly, continues to be so despite a miserable track record. Economic forecasts are always most upbeat, with expectations of even better times ahead, immediately prior to things rolling over, and they remain positive, in the face of clear deterioration, until the next decline is an undoubted fact. One only has to think back to late 2007 and into 2008 for a clear example of this behaviour. The reverse is seen at troughs and again the experience through the end of the GFC illustrated this perfectly. In late 2007 and then again in early

2009 the stock market reversed long before the majority of economic indicators, and virtually the entire universe of economic forecasters, pointed to a reversal.

The futility of hanging on to every news release as a path to investment success has been known for decades. The legendary speculator Jesse Livermore wrote in *How to Trade in Stocks* in the early part of the last century:

It is too difficult to match up world events or current events, or economic events with the movement of the stock market. This is true because the stock market always moves ahead of world events.

The market often moves contrary to apparent common sense and world events, as if it had a mind of its own, designed to fool most people, most of the time. Eventually the truth of why it moved as it did will emerge.

It is therefore foolish to try and anticipate the movement of the market based on current economic news and current events such as: The Purchasing Managers' Report, the Balance of Payments, Consumer Price Index and the Unemployment figures, even the rumour of war, because these are already factored into the market.

*After the market moved it would be rationalised in endless post mortems by the financial pundits and later when the dust had settled, the real economic, political and world events would eventually be brought into focus by historians as to the actual reasons why the market acted as it did. **But, by that time it is too late to make any money.***

It is a comforting idea that somehow cause and effect are present in economics and the stock market, unfortunately history shows that this is not the case. It is far more likely that both the economic data that is released and the movements of the stock market are reflective of something else, the collective "mood" of society. If "social mood" is rising then optimism grows, the economy improves and the stock market rises, however, this movement is observed in the stock market long before it filters through to economic numbers, hence the idea that Jesse Livermore highlighted of the stock market leading the economy.

Golf in general, and particularly the money involved in professional golf, is another reflection of "social mood". A rising "social mood" sees more money flowing into golf at the same time as stock markets are rising and a falling mood, along with struggling markets, will see golf faltering. The results of this include many of the correlations presented in *Bulls, Birdies, Bogeys and Bears*. The same can be said for other sports, however, the very close relationship between golf and business, over such a very long time, results in the "pulses" of both being so remarkably similar, occasionally to an almost spooky extent.

The chapters in this book have illustrated that the relationship and correlation between golf and investing goes far beyond the realms of coincidence and that it is a relationship that, while not peculiar to golf, is probably more powerfully apparent in golf than any other sport. It is also a truly global relationship that is now becoming even more obvious in the developing world.

The introduction stated that *Bulls, Birdies, Bogeys and Bears* is not a "how to" book on golf or investing, nor is it an explanation as to why the link exists between these two great games, and it went on to state that "while the various "pulses" of golf and investing may have moved in an highly correlated manner, their relationship is neither coincidence, nor is it evidence of either one being cause or effect. Rather both are merely symptoms of broader movements in collective social mood."

Exactly what drives "social mood" is an enormous question and beyond the realm of this book, however, it should still be of value for participants in either the golf industry or the investment industry to recognise just how close the relationship is, and there is still ample scope for further research into this special relationship between the two "great games".

For now it is enough to accept that golf is, and always has been a "bull market" sport. It should not be surprising that the leading golfers on the PGA Tour are still winning less than was won in 2000 and 2007 when stock markets made important peaks. It should be clear why the "gender gap" has narrowed somewhat through this more difficult period and it should also not be surprising if, and more likely when, more "cockroaches" are found, during the next bear market, that golf in some way shape or form is found to have been "in the vicinity at the time".

Finally it should be surprising that Europe somehow, in the most unlikely of fashions and against the odds and the markets won the 2012 Ryder Cup. For an explanation as to how this was so one probably has to look at least toward Spain and possibly even further back (and up) to the late Severiano Ballesteros, for an answer.

BIBLIOGRAPHY

Ted Barret, the *Daily Telegraph Golf Chronicle*, Carton 2005

Bryan Burrough and John Helyar, *Barbarians at the Gate*, Harper & Row 1990

Dale Concannon, *The Ryder Cup*, Arum Press 2001

Kevin Cook, *Tommy's Honour*, Harper Collins 2008

Bernard Darwin, *Out of the Rough*, Classics of Golf 2005

Mark Frost, *The Greatest Game Ever Played*, Hyperion 2002

Charles R Geisst, *Wall Street, A History,* Oxford University Press 1997

Ben Hogan, *The Modern Fundamentals of Golf*, Nicholas Kaye 1957

Mark James, *Into the Bear Pit*, Virgin 2000

Liz Kahn, *Tony Jacklin, The Price of Success*, Hamlyn, 1979

Matthew Knight, *The Times Ryder Cup*, Times Books 2006

Jesse Livermore, *How to Trade in Stocks*, McGraw-Hill 2001
(originally published 1940)

Rocco Mediate and John Feinstein, *Are You Kidding me*,
Little, Brown and co, 2009

Robert R. Prechter, Jr. *The Wave Principle of Human Social Behavior and the New Science of Socionomics.* New Classics Library. 1999

Howard Sounes, *The Wicked Game*, Harper 2005

Donald Steel, *The Guinness Book of Golf Facts and Feats*, Guinness 1980

John Steele Gordon, *The Great Game*, Scribner 1999

Herbert Warren Wind, *The Complete Golfer*, Heineman 1955

ACKNOWLEDGEMENTS

Bulls, Birdies, Bogeys and Bears has been a long time in the writing. It was at least eight years ago that I first noticed that the "pulses" bore such an uncanny resemblance, and then the more I observed the progress of the major stock markets of the world the more "echoes" I saw in the world of professional golf, and vice versa. Undoubtedly my primary thanks should go to my family – my wife and golfing buddy, Julia, and our three sons, Thomas, Michael and Jack. It was them that for so long had to tolerate firstly my seemingly perverse joy in finding these echoes but also then had to put up with me assuming that everyone else should find them as incredible as I did. Finally, as the project gained momentum they kindly allowed it to become my overwhelming obsession.

These previously unnoticed relationships were first exposed to a wider public in the form of a regular column in New Zealand's leading golf magazine *The Cut*. I must thank Peter Williams, of TVNZ, firstly for sharing some of my fascination in the relationships and then for his introduction to the team at *The Cut*. I would also like to acknowledge the enthusiasm and support that Heather Kidd and Bob Howitt of *The Cut* gave to my column and more recently to this project.

This is the first book that I have written, however, prior to this I have regularly written many thousands of words a month, for distribution to clients and colleagues, on investment. Through that process I learnt that I have a strong tendency for long sentences and I have to thank Pike Talbert for highlighting this most gently, for his patience in editing all those papers I wrote and for his considered and knowledgeable input into *Bulls, Birdies, Bogeys and Bear*s.

The team at Wilkinson Publishing, and Michael in particular, deserve a very big thank you. I first met Michael a little over a year ago, he was a reader of my monthly *Strategy Thoughts*, a client and I was a Chief Investment Officer, at the end of the meeting I mentioned the idea behind this book and that I had put together a proposal. His interest was clearly genuine and without his support, encouragement and mentoring this project would never have come to fruition.

I must thank my parents who introduced me to golf as an eight or nine year old, none of us realised that it would become such an important part of my life, and finally I have to thank my first boss at Merrill Lynch, John Owen. When John first hired me I was a twenty-one-year-old physics graduate from Magdalen College, Oxford, who as an undergraduate had spent more time playing golf than studying physics. I knew virtually nothing about investment and investment markets. I have always maintained that John had a far better understanding about what I may be good at, and ultimately fascinated by, than I ever did. He was absolutely right, over the last more than thirty years my fascination with investment markets, some would say obsession, has only grown, just as it has with golf.

INDEX